# Investigating Diabetes:
# Real Facts for Real Lives

**Library of Congress Cataloguing-in-Publication Data**

Ambrose, Marylou.
  Investigating diabetes: real facts for real lives / by Marylou Ambrose.
    p. cm.—(Investigating diseases)
  Includes bibliographical references and index.
  Summary: "Provides information about diabetes, including treatment, diagnosis, history, medical advances, and true stories about people with the disease"—Provided by publisher.

  ISBN-13: 978-0-7660-3338-2
  ISBN-10: 0-7660-3338-4

  1. Diabetes—Juvenile literature.  I. Title.
  RC660.5.A43 2010
  616.4'62—dc22

                                                      2008030778

Printed in the United States of America
052010 Lake Book Manufacturing, Inc., Melrose Park, IL

10 9 8 7 6 5 4 3 2 1

**To Our Readers:**
We have done our best to make sure all Internet Addresses in this book were active and appropriate when we went to press. However, the author and the publisher have no control over and assume no liability for the material available on those Internet sites or on other Web sites they may link to. Any comments or suggestions can be sent by e-mail to comments@enslow.com or to the address on the back cover.

♻ Enslow Publishers, Inc., is committed to printing our books on recycled paper. The paper in every book contains 10% to 30% post-consumer waste (PCW). The cover board on the outside of each book contains 100% PCW. Our goal is to do our part to help young people and the environment too!

**Photo Credits:** American Diabetes Association, p. 77; © Andrea Gingerich, p. 120; © Andrew Paul Leonard/Photo Researchers, Inc., p. 111; Animas Corp., p. 88; AP Photo/Dan Steinberg (Berry), p. 21; AP Photo/Peter Kramer (Jonas), p. 21; AP Photo/Tammie Arroyo, p. 22; © Bill Aron/Photo Edit, p. 64; Chris Schmidt, p. 78; Dawn Allynn, p. 114; © Dawna Stafford, p. 141; Eli Lilly, p. 19; © Enslow Publishers, p. 27; © iStock/Aldo Murillo, p. 3; © iStock/Brenda McEwan, p. 104; © iStock/Derek Latta, p. 4; © iStock/Rade Pavlovic, p. 87; © iStock/Richard Cano, p. 85; © iStock/Steve Cole, p. 34; © Jacom Stephens, pp. 71, 124; Jan Roger Johannesen, p. 25; © Jim Kolaczko, p. 129; © Jonathan Selkowitz, p. 10; Karen Barefoot, p. 91; Library of Congress, p. 23; Lifescan, pp. 83, 109; National Dairy Council, p. 68; National Institute of Diabetes and Digestive and Kidney Diseases, National Institutes of Health, pp. 102, 112; © Shutterstock, pp. 31, 62, 97; © Steve Gschmeissner/Photo Researchers, Inc., p. 49; Teodora Vlaicu, p. 24; The Thomas Fisher Rare Book Library, University of Toronto, pp. 50, 52; USDA, p. 67; Veer, p. 72; Vero/Carlo/Photo-Researchers, Inc., p. 15; Wikimedia Commons, pp. 43, 44.

**Cover Photo**: © iStock/Neil Brake

INVESTIGATING
DISEASES

# Investigating Diabetes:
# Real Facts for Real Lives

## Marylou Ambrose

**Enslow Publishers, Inc.**
40 Industrial Road
Box 398
Berkeley Heights, NJ 07922
USA
http://www.enslow.com

# Table of Contents

# What Is Diabetes?

Diabetes is a disease in which the body either fails to make or cannot properly use insulin, the hormone that lets cells take in glucose (sugar) for fuel. Because the cells cannot take in glucose, large amounts of this sugar accumulate in the blood. Several types of diabetes exist. The most common are type 1 and type 2.

### WHAT ARE THE SYMPTOMS?

Diabetes symptoms include extreme thirst, increased urination, lack of energy, a flu-like feeling, weight loss, hunger, blurry vision, sores that heal slowly, frequent infections, red and swollen gums, and tingling or numbness in the fingers, hands, arms, legs, and feet.

### WHAT CAUSES DIABETES?

Causes of type 1 diabetes are uncertain, but heredity and viral infections may contribute to the disease. Type 2 diabetes is mainly caused by heredity, diet, obesity, and lack of exercise.

### HOW MANY PEOPLE HAVE DIABETES?

Worldwide, 246 million people have diabetes; 17.9 to 23.6 million of them live in the United States.

### WHO GETS DIABETES?

Type 1 is seen mainly in children and teenagers; type 2 occurs mainly in adults. However, type 2 is starting to be seen in young people and type 1 in adults. Diabetes occurs in all races, but type 2 is more common in non-whites.

## IS IT CURABLE?

There is no known cure for diabetes. Treatments include insulin injections, change of diet, blood glucose monitoring, and exercise for type 1, and medication, diet, exercise, and sometimes insulin injections for type 2. Pancreas transplants and new, experimental islet cell transplants are also used to treat type 1.

## IS IT PREVENTABLE?

Type 1 diabetes cannot be prevented. Type 2 may be prevented by controlling one's diet, staying at a normal weight, and exercising.

# Introduction

Diabetes is not a high-profile disease. Some people who receive lots of media attention, like actors and athletes, do have it, but they might not talk about it. That is true for most people with the disease. They are too busy living their lives to make a big deal out of diabetes.

But diabetes *is* a big issue. It is the sixth leading cause of death in the United States[1] and the fourth leading cause of death by disease in the world.[2] In 2007, 246 million people worldwide had diabetes[3] and 17.9 to 23.6 million of them were in the United States.[4]

If diabetes is so widespread, why is it still such a mystery to many people? Most know that it has something to do with sugar in the body and that people have to give themselves insulin shots and cannot eat certain foods. Other than that, there's not a lot of public knowledge out there.

This book is for teens who want to learn about diabetes and the people who live with it every day. What happens in the body when someone has diabetes? What are the symptoms? What tests are used to diagnose diabetes and what are they like? How is diabetes treated? Can it be prevented? Cured? What do all those medical words mean? Readers will find the answers to these questions and many more, as well as read stories about real teens and athletes who are meeting the diabetes challenge head on.

# CHAPTER ONE

# The Diabetes Dilemma

## DIABETES AND THE OLYMPIC SKIER

Olympic cross-country skier Kris Freeman was only a year old when his father introduced him to skiing. While his dad skied, he pulled toddler Kris behind him on a sled. When Kris was two, he got up on skis himself, and by the time he was a young teenager, he was competing in cross-country races in his home state of New Hampshire and all over New England.

After attending the University of Vermont for one year, Kris decided his heart was on the slopes, not in the classroom. He had already raced in the Junior World Championships in Switzerland, Austria, and Slovakia, so he decided to postpone his education and become a competitive skier. In 2000, at the age of 20, Kris won the

Kris Freeman didn't let diabetes stand in the way of his Olympic skiing dreams.

30 Kilometer Classic Race, his first national title. He is only the second male cross-country skier from the United States to win a national title as a junior.

Kris was getting ready to train for the 2002 Olympics when he went for a checkup. He was concerned because his vision seemed blurry, he had been thirsty and urinating more than usual, and he was having trouble sleeping. The doctor gave him some news that shook his world: He had type 1 diabetes. "I was told my Olympic-level athletic career was not going to be able to continue, but I wasn't going to go out that easily," he remembers.[1]

All his life, Kris had dreamed of skiing in the Olympics, so even though the doctors were pessimistic, he did not give up. He knew very little about diabetes— no one in his family had it. So he went to the library, did research online, and found out as much as he could about new ways to treat the disease, from better glucose monitors to faster-acting insulins. "I decided the doctors didn't yet know what was possible with these new tools," Kris says.[2]

He went on insulin immediately, learning how to give himself injections, test his blood sugar, and eat the right foods in the right amounts to control his diabetes. "I trained right after being diagnosed," Kris says. "I went kayaking on a reservoir in Park City, Utah. I wasn't going to give up."[3]

Kris was in great physical shape when he entered the 2002 Olympics in Salt Lake City, Utah. He finished 22nd and 15th in two distance races and had the sixth

*Continued on next page*

*Continued from previous page*

fastest time in the team relay. He boosted the United States cross-country team to fifth place—the best the team had ever done in history. In 2006, he entered the winter Olympics in Torino, Italy, along with his older brother, Justin, another cross-country skier. Unfortunately, Kris caught the flu and finished in 22nd place again, although he was expected to do much better. But instead of being discouraged, he just started planning for his next race.

Training for a race takes months. Kris trains up to 6 hours a day for $11\frac{1}{2}$ months a year, logging nearly 1,000 hours of aerobic training a year. When there is no snow on the ground, he kayaks, roller skis (skis on land on special training skis with rollers), and rides a mountain bike.

An athlete with diabetes needs a lot of last-minute preparation, too. Before a race, Kris tests his blood sugar level up to ten times. If it is too low, he drinks a sports drink or eats an energy bar, and if it is too high he injects more insulin. The night before a race, he injects himself with a long-lasting insulin to fuel his muscles for the next day.

"It can be a nuisance leading up to the start of a race," Kris admits. "However, I always start my races with ideal blood sugar. I will not allow diabetes to put me at a disadvantage when I race. The disease is just one more thing I have to deal with in my preparation."[4]

Normally, Kris injects himself with insulin ten times a day. This seems like a lot, but he says, "It's my choice to take insulin ten times a day. If I don't keep super tight control, I don't feel right. The side effects from not taking care of yourself are a lot worse than a pin prick."[5]

While training, he consumes as many as 4,500 calories per day. He plans his food carefully, calculating how many carbohydrates and proteins he needs to balance his workout. During a race, which can be over 30 miles long, he drinks sports drinks while going down hills. In fact, all the racers do this, whether or not they have diabetes. "Our coaches hand us the drinks from the side of the trail," Kris says.[6]

Since the Olympics, Kris has won several national championships and is ranked the number one cross-country skier in the United States and the second most successful American cross-country skier of all time. He has competed all over the world and now has his sights set on the future Olympics. "I'm doing everything I can to get a medal," he says.[7]

During his off season, Kris is a spokesperson for Eli Lilly, a drug company that produces diabetes medications. He travels around the country as the LillyforLife program ambassador. He visits diabetes expos and summer camps for children with diabetes to talk to them about their condition and inspire them to lead healthy lives. He tells them: "Believe in yourself and everything is possible. Nothing can stop you."[8]

Kris refused to let diabetes throw his skiing career off track. But like other successful athletes with diabetes, he takes the disease very seriously. He visits his doctor regularly and is meticulous about eating right, testing his blood sugar, and taking insulin. This keeps him at peak performance level both on the ski trails and off.

Everyone with diabetes needs to take the disease very seriously. Why? Because diabetes can cause devastating complications, such as blindness, kidney failure, or heart disease if it is ignored or taken lightly. It can even be fatal. Luckily, there are many healthy behaviors and medicines that can help people with diabetes stay well and live long lives.

## A SUGAR "HIGH"

Diabetes is sometimes called "sugar diabetes" or the "sugar disease" because it occurs when the delicate system that controls the amount of sugar (glucose) in the bloodstream gets out of balance.

### The Name Game

The full name of diabetes is *diabetes mellitus*, pronounced "die-uh-BEE-teez MEL-uh-tus." The name *diabetes* comes from the Greek verb "to straddle" or "cross over" like a siphon. (A siphon is a U-shaped tube used to transfer liquid from a higher container to a lower one.) It was used by the second-century Greek physician Aretaeus the Cappadocian, who noticed that some of his patients drank large amounts of fluids and urinated so frequently, they were like siphons. In 1674, the British physician Thomas Willis actually tasted his patients' urine! He noticed it was sweet and added the Latin word "mellitus," (which means "honey sweet") to further describe the puzzling disease.

Glucose is the body's main source of energy. Carbohydrates (starches and sugars) are turned into glucose in the small intestine. Then the glucose passes through the intestine into the bloodstream, where it travels to cells in the muscles, organs, and other tissues and is used as fuel.

The amount of glucose or sugar in the blood is controlled by a hormone called insulin. Insulin is produced in the pancreas, a large organ located behind the stomach. In diabetes, the pancreas either stops making insulin or does not make enough insulin,

Insulin is produced in the pancreas (shown in red), a large organ behind the stomach.

or the body does not use the insulin effectively. So glucose stays in the bloodstream, where it accumulates to dangerous levels. High blood glucose can cause extreme thirst, frequent urination, weight loss, and other symptoms. Over time, it can also damage organs and tissues, causing serious, even deadly, consequences.

## WHO GETS DIABETES?

Diabetes strikes people of both sexes, and all ages, races, and ethnic backgrounds. Each year, 3.8 million people worldwide die from complications of diabetes, making it the fourth leading cause of death by disease. Every ten seconds, two people somewhere in the world develop diabetes and one person dies from diabetes-related causes.[9]

Scientists are still investigating what causes type 1 diabetes. They have found that people who have family members with the disease are more likely to get it themselves. Some scientists think a virus triggers the disease, but this is still being studied.

We know a lot more about the causes of type 2 diabetes. The chance of developing a disease is called a risk. Having a close family member with the disease also raises the risk for type 2 diabetes, but being overweight and inactive are just as risky.

The following things will *not* give a person diabetes:

- Being around someone with diabetes
- Eating sugar
- Being stressed out

## WHY IS DIABETES SO COMMON?

In 1985, about 30 million people worldwide had diabetes. Today, an alarming 246 million people have it.[10] Even more alarming, a growing number of children and teens are developing type 2 diabetes, which used to be seen mostly in people over age 45.

Why is type 2 diabetes on the rise? Chalk it up to being overweight and inactive—both risk factors for diabetes. Call it a side effect of our modern lifestyle.

A century ago, most people still grew or cooked their own food. They ate homegrown fruits and vegetables and home-baked breads that did not come in packages loaded with sugar and other additives. Today, food is convenient and plentiful, but it is often unhealthy, too.

In addition, the work of harvesting the food has been replaced by a quick drive to the supermarket or fast food restaurant. In the old days, getting food, making food, and accomplishing everyday tasks took lots of work. Who needed a gym? Just getting through the day was plenty of exercise. Today, exercise is a choice, and although it should be considered a necessity, it often is not.

About one in three adults in America is overweight or obese. In children and teens, 13.9 percent are overweight in the 2-to-5 age group, 18.8 percent are overweight in the 6-to-11 age group, and 17.4 percent are overweight in the 12-to-19 age group. (Obesity is extreme overweight—over 30 percent body fat for

## The Glucose Breakdown

What starts as a bite of an apple or a chocolate donut gets digested (broken down) into miniscule molecules before they pass through the lining of the small intestine and enter the bloodstream. The proteins, carbohydrates, and fats from food each require special intestinal juices to break them into molecules. Proteins are broken down into amino acids and fats into fatty acids—both small enough to enter the bloodstream.

When carbohydrates—like bread, cereal, honey, or fruit—reach the small intestine, they break down into simple sugars, mainly glucose. Once glucose is in the blood, it is carried to each cell, where it is used to generate the body's energy and build new cells, or stored in the liver as glycogen. The amount of glucose in the blood is called the blood sugar level or blood glucose level and is measured in milligrams per deciliter or mg/dl (a deciliter is one-tenth of a liter).

adults—while being overweight means that an adult has between 25 and 29.9 percent body fat.) Compared to 20 years ago, three times as many American children are overweight or obese.[11] These statistics are especially distressing because no matter what one's age, being overweight or obese can contribute to the development of type 2 diabetes.

## ARE THERE COMPLICATIONS?

People with diabetes cannot take good health for granted—they have to work to achieve it. This involves testing their blood glucose levels, being careful about what they eat, staying at a healthy weight, exercising regularly, and either injecting insulin or taking medication (sometimes doing both). If they are vigilant about taking care of their diabetes, they will usually remain healthy.

But suppose a person had diabetes and did not follow his or her doctor's orders? The consequences are frightening. If blood glucose gets too high or too low, a diabetic could have seizures, lose consciousness, go into a coma, or even die. There are also many complications that can arise in someone who has been living with diabetes for a while and does not realize he or she has it. Complications include problems with the heart and circulatory system, kidneys, nerves, eyes, skin, teeth, and feet. These problems usually can be treated, but preventing them is a much better course of action.

## What Is Insulin?

Many people with diabetes have to inject themselves with a substance called insulin to stay healthy. Insulin is a hormone produced by the pancreas. Hormones are chemical substances our bodies make that control the function of certain cells or organs. Insulin controls how much glucose or sugar the liver produces. It also helps move glucose from the bloodstream into the cells where it is used for energy. Without insulin, glucose cannot get into the cells, so it accumulates in the blood. Too much glucose causes the eyes, kidneys, nerves, and many other organs and tissues to deteriorate. That is why people with diabetes need to replace their insulin with shots or take medicine to encourage the pancreas to produce more insulin.

Products such as Humalog allow people with diabetes to replace their body's insulin with shots.

## LIVING WITH DIABETES

Although diabetes is incurable, people with the disease can lead active lives and pursue careers. Many movie stars, musicians, and professional athletes are living successfully with diabetes. So are people we come into contact with every day–teachers, parents of friends, other students, the clerk at the grocery store, the nurse at the doctor's office, and on and on.

Diabetes is so common that most people unknowingly cross paths every day with someone who has the disease.

That is because most people with diabetes are coping very well and living happy, healthy lives without making a big deal out of their illness.

Of course, in many ways, diabetes *is* a serious issue. It takes time, effort, and determination to live well with this disease. People must educate themselves about diabetes and understand it, learn how to give themselves injections and test their blood glucose, learn which foods to eat and which ones to avoid, and much more. But eventually, these tasks become second nature.

Olympic cross-country skier Kris Freeman puts it this way: "It's what I have to do. You get used to it. I probably spend about five minutes a day dealing with the disease."[12]

No one wants to have diabetes. But the upside to this disease is that people learn a great deal about nutrition and exercise, start leading healthier lifestyles, and begin "listening" to their bodies.

## CELEBRITIES WITH DIABETES[13]

| NAME | OCCUPATION |
| --- | --- |
| Halle Berry | Movie actress |
| James Cagney | Legendary movie actor |
| Thomas Edison | Inventor |
| Ernest Hemingway | 20th-century novelist |
| Jerry Garcia | Lead singer of The Grateful Dead |
| Jackie Gleason | Comedian |
| Mikhail Gorbachev | Former Soviet premier |
| Mike Huckabee | Arkansas governor & 2008 presidential candidate |
| Howard Hughes | Industrialist |
| Nicole Johnson | Miss America in 1999 |
| Nick Jonas | Musician, member of the Jonas Brothers |

| | |
|---|---|
| Ray Kroc | Founder of McDonald's fast food restaurants |
| Tommy Lee | Drummer for Motley Crüe |
| Jerry Mathers | Child star of *Leave It to Beaver* |
| Mary Tyler Moore | TV and movie actress |
| Carroll O'Connor | Star of *All in the Family* |
| Pope John Paul II | Catholic religious leader (1920–2005) |
| Elvis Presley | Rock 'n' roll icon |
| Mario Puzo | Author of *The Godfather* (book and movies) |
| Anne Rice | Author of *Interview with a Vampire* |
| Sharon Stone | Actress |
| Aida Turturro | Actress on *The Sopranos* |
| Vanessa Williams | Singer, actress on *Ugly Betty* |

## ATHLETES WITH DIABETES[14]

| NAME | SPORT |
|------|-------|
| Jay Hewitt | Ironman triathlete |
| Chris Dudley | Basketball player, New York Knicks |
| Jonathan Hayes | Football player, coach for Cincinnati Bengals |
| Scott Verplank | Golfer, number 16 on 2005 PGA Tour Money List |
| Scott Dunton | World class professional surfer |
| Will Cross | Expeditioner, climbed Mount Everest in 2005 |
| Gary Hall, Jr. | Olympic gold medalist in swimming |
| Bobby Clarke | Ice hockey player, Philadelphia Flyers |
| Ty Cobb | Legendary baseball player |
| Billy Jean King | Tennis player |
| Evel Knievel | Daredevil |

# CHAPTER TWO

# The Science of Diabetes

Diabetes is a disease of sugar metabolism. The way the body handles sugar becomes abnormal. And most people eat a lot of sugar—probably too much.

According to the United States Department of Agriculture (USDA), the average American consumes 152 pounds of caloric sweeteners a year, or about 32 teaspoons a day. This includes table sugar plus the added sugar and high-fructose corn syrup that are in foods like cereals, candy, and soft drinks. It does not take into account the sugar found naturally in fruit and other foods.

The USDA says we should be consuming about 10 teaspoons of sugar a day, equal to the amount in one 12-ounce can of soda.[1] But we all know people who chug two or three colas or energy drinks a day and never seem to pass a convenience store without stopping for a candy bar.

Not all sugar is bad. Tasty desserts are okay—in moderation, with careful attention to blood sugar monitoring.

Studies show that sugar consumption in the United States has been increasing steadily since the 1980s, right along with obesity rates.[2] So it comes as no surprise that type 2 diabetes, which is partly caused by obesity, is also reaching epidemic proportions.

So all sugar is bad, right? Wrong. Desserts and sugary snacks and cereals are fine in moderation. The white, brown, or confectioners' sugar added to these foods is called sucrose. Many foods also contain natural sugars. For example, fruit and honey contain fructose, milk and milk products contain lactose, and grains contain maltose. Sugar is everywhere, and trying to banish it from our diets would be both unrealistic and unhealthy.

## Blood tests

**Testing blood glucose is very important in diabetes treatment.** According to the American Diabetes Association, normal fasting glucose levels are less than 100 mg/dl. In prediabetes, levels are 100 to 125 mg/dl. Readings above 126 mg/dl indicate diabetes.

A blood glucose meter measures and digitally displays a person's blood glucose level.

All people have some sugar in their blood. But in diabetes, the body's system for converting sugar into fuel gets seriously out of balance. Instead of moving sugar to the cells, sugar builds up in the bloodstream, reaching critical levels.

To understand what goes wrong in diabetes, we must first understand how the body handles sugar in a person without diabetes.

## HOW DIGESTION WORKS

During digestion, food is transformed into tiny molecules of nutrients that enter the bloodstream and travel to all cells in the body. Some foods are changed into a sugar called glucose. Glucose is the fuel that energizes all the cells, tissues, and organs in the body, including those in the brain, heart, liver, and other vital organs. Without glucose, these organs would stop working.

Glucose comes from starches, such as bread, pasta, cereal, and corn, and from foods containing natural sugars, such as fruit, yogurt, and milk, as well as soft drinks, cake, candy, and other snack foods that have sugar added to them. All these foods are classified as carbohydrates.

Imagine eating a slice of bread. After you chew and swallow it, the small pieces travel to the stomach, where they mix with digestive juices. Then the stomach slowly empties its contents into the small intestine, where the molecules of bread mix with more digestive juices. What was once a slice of bread has now been converted to a simple sugar called glucose that is so small, it can pass through the walls of the intestine and enter the bloodstream.

## THE INSULIN/GLUCOSE PARTNERSHIP

Once in the bloodstream, glucose travels throughout the body to nourish the cells, tissues, and organs. But it needs the help of insulin to do this. Insulin is a hormone produced in the pancreas, an organ located behind the stomach. The pancreas senses when glucose levels rise in the blood and reacts by signaling its beta cells to release insulin into the bloodstream. The beta cells are located in a part of the pancreas called the islets of Langerhans. Once in the blood, insulin hurries to the cells and attaches to them, preparing the cells to welcome glucose with open arms. Think of insulin as the doorman at the entrance to the cells. Insulin opens the door and ushers glucose in. When glucose enters the cells, it finally can be used as fuel for the body's vital organs and tissues.

Pancreas makes insulin (I) and sends it into the bloodstream.

Sugar (S) enters the bloodstream from food or drink.

Receptor

Cell

Insulin "unlocks" the cell so sugar can get in.

With no insulin as the key, sugar can't get in.

**Insulin regulates cells' uptake of sugar.**

    Insulin is a busy hormone. You see, glucose does not just come from food. It is also stored as glycogen in the liver, a large organ in the upper abdomen. When needed, the liver turns glycogen back to glucose and releases it to provide sugar for energy between meals and during sleep. Insulin not only regulates how cells take up glucose, it also affects how much glucose the liver releases from its glycogen storage.

## WHAT GOES WRONG IN DIABETES?

When a person has diabetes, serious problems occur when glucose leaves the small intestine and enters the bloodstream. Either there is no insulin to tell the cells to take in sugar because the pancreas has stopped producing insulin (type 1 diabetes) or the body does not react to the insulin normally and only lets a little glucose into the cells (type 2 diabetes).

Either way, glucose builds up in the bloodstream, is filtered out by the kidneys, and flushes out of the body in the urine, without performing its job as the body's main source of fuel. It leaves the cells starved for energy and causes major health problems. Why does this happen? The reasons depend on the type of diabetes a person has.

## TYPES OF DIABETES

The two most common types of diabetes are type 1 and type 2. Several less-common types also exist: gestational diabetes, adult onset-variety of type 1, maturity-onset diabetes of the young (MODY), and hybrid diabetes. All six types cause blood glucose levels to become higher than normal.

### Type 1 Diabetes

Type 1 diabetes used to be called juvenile diabetes, because half of the people diagnosed with it are children or teenagers. It was also once called insulin-dependent diabetes, because people with this type of diabetes must take insulin to stay healthy. Type 1 diabetes usually occurs before age 30 and generally comes on suddenly. Five to 10 percent of all known cases of diabetes are type 1,[3] and the disease affects 900,000 to 1.8 million Americans.[4] So far, there is no cure for type 1 diabetes. People must take insulin injections to keep their blood glucose levels down and stay healthy.

Type 1 diabetes arises when the pancreas loses its ability to make insulin. Why does this occur? Researchers still are not entirely sure. They know heredity plays a part because people whose parents or grandparents have type 1 diabetes often have it, too. On the other hand, many people with type 1 diabetes have no family history of the disease.

Some experts believe that a viral infection might trigger type 1 diabetes, but only in people who are already susceptible to the disease because their family members have it. The body's immune system can become flawed, and instead of attacking the virus it might attack the pancreas and destroy the beta cells that produce insulin instead. But although several studies have been conducted, no specific virus has been identified.

In a study done in England, scientists looked at the medical records of more than 4,000 people under age 30 who had type 1 diabetes. All the people had lived in Yorkshire between 1978 and 2002. The study found that new cases of type 1 diabetes cropped up in groups of young people aged 10 to 19 who all lived in certain sections of Yorkshire. The researchers concluded that something encountered in the Yorkshire environment, possibly an infection or a virus, might well have caused these type 1 diabetes cases.[5]

## What Is Autoimmunity?

The body's immune system protects against infections and other diseases by producing protein molecules called antibodies. The antibodies' job is to circulate in the body and identify, attack, and destroy any foreign invaders, such as viruses or bacteria.

But sometimes, the immune system gets confused, thinks the body's own tissues or organs are foreign, and attacks them. This is called autoimmunity. Type 1 diabetes is an autoimmune disease because the immune system attacks the beta cells in the pancreas, destroying them so they can never make insulin again.

Other autoimmune diseases include multiple sclerosis (a nerve disease), rheumatoid arthritis (a joint disease), and vitiligo (a skin disease).

So far, type 1 diabetes cannot be prevented, but researchers continue to search for ways to ward off the disease in susceptible people.

How do you know if you have type 1 diabetes? Common symptoms are urinating frequently, being thirsty all the time, being unusually hungry but still losing weight, feeling abnormally tired, and having blurry vision.

Why do these symptoms happen? Frequent urination occurs because the kidneys are working overtime. Their job is to sift out waste products from the blood and also get rid of excess water. The waste products and extra water become urine. When too much sugar accumulates in the blood, it gets flushed out in the urine, too, causing the kidneys to work harder than normal and produce more urine. That is why people with diabetes have to make so many trips to the bathroom.

It also explains why people with diabetes are so thirsty—losing so much fluid makes them drink more to avoid dehydration (excessive water loss). Blurry vision is due to swelling of the lens inside the eye because it absorbs glucose and water from the blood.

Hunger occurs because fats, vitamins, minerals, and protein are flushed out in the excess urine. But even though a person eats more, he still loses weight because the body can't use the glucose in the bloodstream as fuel. Instead, it uses its own muscle and stored fat. Tiredness occurs because the body cannot use glucose properly for energy.

People with untreated diabetes are very thirsty—unusually so.

## Type 2 Diabetes

Type 2 diabetes was formerly called adult-onset diabetes because it is usually diagnosed in adulthood. It was also once called non-insulin-dependent diabetes because it does not always require insulin injections and can sometimes be treated with diet, weight loss, and pills to lower glucose levels.

## Knock, Knock, Who's There?

When glucose enters the bloodstream, the pancreas senses this and releases insulin. Glucose heads for the cells but insulin gets there first and attaches itself to the cells. Insulin is the "doorman" that opens the door to the cells and lets glucose in. In people with diabetes, the pancreas either doesn't produce enough insulin or the body doesn't respond to the insulin normally. So glucose builds up in the blood because not much can enter the cells.

Type 2 diabetes is much more common than type 1 diabetes. Ninety to 95 percent of all people with diabetes in the United States have type 2. It is more common in older people; in fact, 18 percent of those over age 60 have it.[6] However, obesity and lack of exercise are causing some children and teens to get type 2 diabetes, too.

Once a person is diagnosed with type 2 diabetes, there is no known cure. But the disease can often be prevented or treated through diet, exercise, and other lifestyle changes, as well as by taking medicine to lower blood glucose levels. Some people also require insulin injections.

Unlike people with type 1 diabetes, those with type 2 diabetes *do* produce insulin in the pancreas. But for some reason, their bodies do not react to insulin normally. So when insulin attaches itself to the cells and tries to open the door for glucose to enter, the cells resist and only let some glucose in. This condition is called insulin resistance. Eventually, blood glucose levels rise, prompting the pancreas to make even more insulin in an attempt to get glucose out of the blood and into the cells. Finally, the pancreas exhausts itself. It gets worn out and can no longer keep up with the body's increasing demands for insulin.

Insulin resistance leads to a condition called prediabetes, where blood glucose levels are higher than normal but still not high enough to be called diabetes. At least 54 million Americans have prediabetes and are very likely to develop type 2 diabetes within 10 years if they do not change their exercise and eating habits. If a person who weighs 200 pounds loses just 10 to 15 pounds and walks 30 minutes a day, this is often enough to fight off diabetes.[7]

What causes type 2 diabetes is not a mystery. Risks (things that increase the chance of developing a disease) are discussed in more detail in Chapter 4, but they include the following:

- A family history of diabetes
- Belonging to one of the following minority groups: Latinos, African Americans, and some Native Americans and Asians
- Being overweight, especially with extra abdominal fat
- Not exercising
- Being over age 45
- Having prediabetes
- Having had gestational diabetes (diabetes only when pregnant)
- Having certain diseases, such as Addison's Disease
- Taking steroids

Type 2 diabetes takes many years to develop and symptoms may occur so gradually that people do not even notice them. They may visit their doctor for their yearly checkup and then find out they have type 2 diabetes when a routine blood test reveals high blood glucose levels.

WARNING SIGNS OF DIABETES

People with type 1 or type 2 diabetes may have some or all of these symptoms:

- Extreme thirst
- Increased urination
- Lack of energy, flu-like feeling
- Weight loss even though they eat a lot
- Blurry vision
- Skin sores that heal slowly
- Frequent infections; yeast or bladder infections in women
- Red, swollen, tender gums
- Tingling, numbness, or burning pain in the fingers, hands, arms, legs, and feet

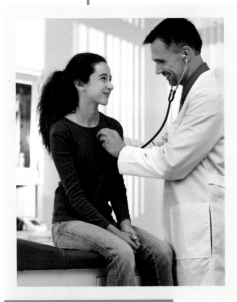

Doctors can help patients deal with managing many aspects of chronic diseases such as diabetes.

People who do not have diabetes often experience one or more of these symptoms sometime in their lives. But when several of these symptoms occur at once and do not get better, it is time to see a doctor.

Without treatment, these people will eventually have some of the same symptoms as in type 1 diabetes: unquenchable thirst, increased urination, blurred vision, fatigue, and weight loss. Luckily, these problems go away with proper treatment.

---

OTHER TYPES OF DIABETES

Besides type 1, type 2, and gestational diabetes, three other types of diabetes have been discovered.

**Hybrid or mixed diabetes:** Some children and teens show symptoms of both type 1 and type 2 diabetes. This occurs when a child with type 1 diabetes becomes overweight and develops insulin resistance (as in type 2 diabetes), or when a child with type 2 diabetes develops antibodies against the beta cells that produce insulin (as in type 1 diabetes).

Most people with hybrid diabetes need insulin injections, but they may also take medications to reduce insulin resistance. Exercise, healthy eating, losing weight, and keeping blood sugar levels close to normal are also a must. Some studies show that 15 to 20 percent of teens with type 2 diabetes also have symptoms of type 1 diabetes.[8]

**Maturity-onset diabetes of the young (MODY):** This rare type of diabetes occurs in children, teens, and young adults. A gene defect harms insulin production. Insulin resistance is usually not present.

*Continued on next page*

*Continued from previous page*

The disease is hereditary, and children who have one parent with MODY have a 50 percent chance of inheriting it. Only 2 to 5 percent of all people with diabetes have MODY, and the disease is often mistaken for type 1 diabetes in children. Treatment varies. Some people do well with diet, exercise, and medication. Others may need insulin.[9]

**Latent autoimmune diabetes in adults (LADA):** Cases of type 1 diabetes are now being found in adults. At first, people have symptoms of type 2 diabetes, even though they are often active and thin. They also may not have much insulin resistance, the main symptom of type 2 diabetes. But like type 2 patients, they still have some healthy beta cells to produce insulin. Unfortunately, this only lasts a few years and they eventually need insulin injections. Some experts believe that many people diagnosed with type 2 diabetes actually have LADA.

## COMPLICATIONS OF DIABETES

When blood sugar levels get above normal, the body's blood vessels can eventually go haywire. They do things like clog up, get very narrow, or get so weak they leak blood. This decreases the amount of blood that gets to the heart, nerves, eyes, and other organs. Over time, it can cause serious complications. The good news is that some of these complications usually do not occur until years, even decades, after people first learn they have diabetes. Even better news is that keeping blood glucose levels close to normal can prevent or delay the following complications.

## Cardiovascular Disease

This includes problems with the heart and circulatory system. People with diabetes are very susceptible to atherosclerosis—a buildup of fatty deposits in the arteries. These deposits, called plaque, harden and cause the arteries to get narrow or clog up completely, reducing blood supply to the organs. When no blood can reach the heart, or when a plaque ruptures, a heart attack occurs. A stroke occurs when the blood supply to the brain is cut off or a blood vessel bursts. Compared to people without diabetes, adults with diabetes are two to four times more likely to get heart disease and five times more likely to have a stroke.[10] Of course, controlling blood sugar is only one of several ways to prevent cardiovascular disease—others include not smoking, lowering cholesterol levels, lowering blood pressure, and exercising.

## Eye Damage

Diabetes can damage the miniscule blood vessels that transport blood to the retina. (The retina is the part of the eye that transmits visual images to the brain.) Diabetes specifically causes blood vessels in the eye to either get weak or multiply, causing blood to leak into the eye. Called diabetic retinopathy, this condition can result in blurry vision or even blindness if it goes untreated. Almost all people with type 1 diabetes eventually develop retinopathy, and almost three-fourths of people with type 2 diabetes do.[11] Luckily, if it is discovered early enough, it can be delayed or stopped altogether. Controlling blood sugar and getting a yearly eye examination are important ways to prevent this problem; so are lowering blood pressure and not smoking.

### Kidney Disease

The kidneys work 24 hours a day to rid the body of waste products that accumulate in the bloodstream. Tiny blood vessels called capillaries act as filters, but diabetes can damage them. This causes waste products to remain in the blood and nutrients to get flushed out with urine. This problem (called nephropathy) takes years to develop and, unfortunately, most people do not notice symptoms until 80 percent of their kidneys are damaged. About 30 percent of diabetics develop nephropathy.[12] However, controlling blood sugar, taking medications for high blood pressure (if necessary), cutting back on protein, and having urine and kidney tests will help identify and prevent this problem.

### Nerve Damage

High glucose levels can slow down or stop blood flow to the nerves, causing them to stop sending messages, send them at the wrong times, or send them too slowly. This problem is called neuropathy. Depending on which nerves are affected, people may have tingling, numbness, and pain in their hands, legs, and feet; trouble controlling their bladders or bowels; and weak muscles. Men may have trouble getting erections. Sixty to 70 percent of people with diabetes have mild to severe neuropathy, but watching their glucose levels carefully can reduce the risk up to 60 percent.[13] Other preventive measures include not smoking, not drinking alcohol, and exercising regularly.

## Infections

White blood cells defend the body against invading bacteria, viruses, and fungi that can cause infections. But extra glucose in the blood not only weakens the white blood cells, it also looks like a feast to the "invaders." People with diabetes are especially prone to infections in their skin, gums, ears, lungs, skin, feet, genital areas, and in the incision areas after surgery. Serious gum disease is a problem for about one-third of people with diabetes. Infections in the feet are another common problem and can occur when the legs and feet become numb from neuropathy and people do not realize they have an injury. Infections in the feet or legs that are not treated can become so severe that amputation (surgical removal) of the infected part may be necessary to keep the infection from spreading.

Gum infections can be prevented by brushing and flossing teeth daily and visiting the dentist at least every six months. Feet should be checked every day for injuries. Because people with diabetes get a lot sicker from flu, pneumonia, and other infectious diseases than other people, everyone with diabetes should get a yearly flu shot, and all adults with the disease should get a one-time pneumonia vaccine. Teens and young adults should also get the meningococcemia vaccine.

## Kamaal and Malcolm: Creating Diabetes Superheroes

Most kids just diagnosed with type 1 diabetes are preoccupied with getting shots. But not Kamaal Washington. Sure, it was a shock to find out he had diabetes, and he had to get over his fear of needles fast. But while still in the hospital, the 9-year-old had a brainstorm: What if he and his younger brother, Malcolm, created a comic book to teach kids and grownups about diabetes?

Kamaal did not pull this idea out of thin air. His father, Alonzo, is a professional comic book writer, illustrator, and social activist in Kansas City, Missouri. He publishes Omega 7 Comics, which use fantasy to deal with illegal drugs, crime, missing children, and other serious issues. When the boys told their father they wanted to create a comic series about diabetes, he was all for it. The written information they had received in the hospital was hard enough for adults to understand, let alone children. Kamaal figured maybe a comic book would get the point across better.

Right after his diagnosis, Kamaal felt frustrated and overwhelmed. Who could blame him? To make both of them feel stronger, Alonzo would tell Kamaal, "You are not going to let diabetes overcome you. You are going to overcome diabetes."[14] Hearing this, Kamaal knew what message his comics should convey: You can be a hero against diabetes, you can overcome this disease, and you can be a winner.

So far, Kamaal and Malcolm have published two comic books and are planning a third. The books feature Omega Boy, a time-traveling superhero, Mighty Boy, a modern day crime fighter, and Dr. Diabetes, an angry villain who represents the wrong way of dealing with the illness. The boys do the illustrations and Alonzo helps them with the writing. Their comic books have won awards and earned them thousands of dollars, half of which they have donated to diabetes causes.

Kamaal, now age 14, and Malcolm, age 12, have become true diabetes activists. They travel around the country speaking about diabetes, and Kamaal was the Juvenile Diabetes Research Foundation's delegate to the Children's Congress, where he and other kids testified before the U.S. Senate to get more money for diabetes research.[15]

In the future, Kamaal and Malcolm would like to do TV commercials and an animated movie about diabetes. Alonzo hopes they will continue speaking out about diabetes when they become adults.

"If it weren't for my dad, the comic book wouldn't exist, because he's really the one who inspired me to do it," Kamaal said.[16]

# CHAPTER THREE

# The History of Diabetes

D iabetes is far from a new disease. Even the ancient Egyptians had it. The first written record of diabetes can be found in an Egyptian medical document called the Ebers Papyrus, written around 1552 B.C. The 110-page scroll is the oldest medical document on record and contains hundreds of formulas and cures for problems like crocodile bites, burns, fractures, and even psychiatric disorders.

Although there was no name for diabetes then, the Ebers Papyrus describes a condition marked by excessive urination. Patients were noted to suffer from extreme thirst, weight loss, boils, and infections.

In 400 B.C., Indian physician Susrata described a malady that caused excessive urination, which he blamed on gluttony, especially eating too much rice, flour, and sugar. Early descriptions of diabetes describe a disease in which patients passed large amounts of honey-sweet urine, which attracted flies and ants. In fact, one ancient way to diagnose diabetes was to pour urine near an anthill. If the ants swarmed over the anthill, the urine obviously contained sugar, and the patient was ruled to have diabetes.

## "CURES" FOR DIABETES

The expression "the cure is worse than the disease" certainly applies to many early diabetes remedies. Some were terrible, some comical, and all failed. Here is a sampling:

**1500 B.C.:** Fruits, grains, and honey.

**230 B.C.:** Endive, lettuce, herbs, dark-colored wine, and dates (in the first stages of the disease); rose oil, vinegar, and navelwort poultices (moist heat packs) over the kidneys (in the later stages of disease); bleeding (cutting of veins to release blood); avoidance of diuretics (substances that increase urine production).

**47–117 A.D.:** Watered-down wine.

**1000 A.D.:** Horseback riding, emetics (substances that cause vomiting), and sudorifics (substances that cause sweating); cool baths and fragrant wine in the later stages; avoidance of diuretic foods and drugs.

**17th century:** Either eating a lot of sugar or restricting sugar and other carbohydrates; eating only milk, barley, water, and bread.

**18th century:** Bloodletting, drugging patients, overfeeding to make up for the loss of fluids in urine.

**19th century:** Eating large amounts of sugar or starvation diets of less than 500 calories a day. Patients were sometimes locked in their rooms to prevent them from eating.

Bloodletting was a common treatment for diabetes and many other ailments in the Middle Ages.

*Continued on next page*

*Continued from previous page*

**1900–1915:** "Oat cure," "milk diet," "rice cure," and "potato therapy," in which patients ate mostly one food. Opium was also used.

**1921:** A starvation diet to decrease the strain of not being able to use food properly. This diet kept some people alive long enough to be helped by insulin, which was invented in 1922.

Five hundred years later, in the second century A.D., the name "diabetes" was coined by Greek physician Aretaeus. In his records, Aretaeus described diabetes in these words:

Diabetes is a dreadful affliction, not very frequent among men, being a melting down of the flesh and limbs into urine. The patients never stop making water and the flow is incessant, like the opening of aqueducts. Life is short, unpleasant and painful, thirst unquenchable, drinking excessive, and disproportionate to the large quantity of urine, for yet more urine is passed . . . the patients are affected by nausea, restlessness and burning thirst, and within a short time they expire.[1]

Although ancient physicians could describe the outward signs of diabetes, they had no idea how to treat it effectively or ease patients' suffering.

Greek physician Aretaeus coined the term "diabetes" in the second century A.D.

## THE DARK AGES AND BEYOND

During the Dark Ages (476 to 1000 A.D.), progress toward diagnosing diabetes was at a standstill. One interesting practice during this time was employing "water tasters" to sample the urine of people suspected of having diabetes! If the urine tasted sweet, they were thought to have the disease.

Unbelievably, this crude diagnostic method was still being used centuries later by doctors trying desperately to unlock the mystery of diabetes. In 1674, Thomas Willis, a doctor in Oxford, England, tasted his diabetic patients' urine and recorded that it tasted sweet and thus contained sugar.

> One interesting practice during this time was employing "water tasters" to sample the urine of people suspected of having diabetes! If the urine tasted sweet, they were thought to have the disease.

In 1709, Swiss physician Johann Brunner removed the pancreases from laboratory dogs and discovered that the animals suffered from intense thirst and excessive urination. But although he was on the right track, he was unable to find a connection between the pancreas and diabetes.

Sixty-seven years later, in 1776, British physician Mathew Dobson gently heated two quarts of urine from a patient with diabetes until it was reduced to a dry, whitish, crumbly cake. He described it as smelling "sweet like brown sugar" and also tasting like sugar except for "a slight sense of coolness on the palate."[2] He reinforced what Willis had shown more than 100 years earlier—that sugar was present in the urine. He also observed that an excess of sugar was present in the blood of people with diabetes, proving that diabetes was a disorder involving the whole body, not just the kidneys. This discovery led scientists to suspect that glucose travels from the blood to the urine, but they had no idea how this happened.

Mercifully, in 1791, German physician Johann Peter Frank developed a yeast test to detect sugar in urine. Taste testing finally became a thing of the past.

A major discovery occurred in 1788, when Thomas Crawley of London was the first researcher to discover a definite link between the pancreas and diabetes. After dissecting the pancreas of a patient who had died of diabetes, he saw that the pancreatic tissues were damaged. However, it took another hundred years for scientists to fully understand the significance of this finding.

Another important researcher in the late eighteenth century was Scottish physician John Rollo, the surgeon general of the Royal Artillery. In 1797, he pioneered the idea that limiting certain foods was a treatment for diabetes. After observing patients for many years, he decided that a diet high in meat (fat and protein) was most effective because it produced less sugar in the urine. This started a trend toward high-fat, high-protein, low-carbohydrate diets for diabetes that lasted, with some changes, until the 1920s. This diet actually prolonged the life of some adults by a few years, but it did not help young patients, who usually died a few months after developing diabetes.

In reality, patients on this diet probably improved because they were eating fewer calories, not more protein. This phenomenon was observed by French physician Apollinaire Bouchardat during the Franco-Prussian War of 1870 to 1871. He noticed that the scarcity of food in Paris coincided with a decreased amount of sugar in the urine of his patients with diabetes.

Strides were being made, but the doctors still did not know what malfunction in the body caused diabetes. Was it the blood, kidneys, liver, stomach, or pancreas? In 1857, Claude Bernard, a French physician, discovered that blood sugar levels were affected by a starch-like substance released by the liver. He named this substance "glucogen" and theorized that an excess of it caused diabetes. This was the first time the liver had been associated with diabetes.

## THE PANCREAS TAKES PRIORITY

In 1869, Paul Langerhans, a German medical student, published a paper describing his discovery of "heaps of cells" in the pancreas, which he thought resembled islands.[3] Unfortunately, he died in 1888, before scientists realized the importance of his discovery. The cells were later named the "islets of Langerhans," and spurred scientists around the world to start searching for the "antidiabetic substance" they were sure these cells contained.

Twenty years later, two German physicians, Oscar Minkowski and Joseph von Mering, were conducting experiments to see if the pancreas was involved in the digestion of fats. They decided that removing the pancreas from a laboratory dog was the best way to find out. After the operation, the doctors were astonished to find that the dog urinated over and over. Not only that, but flies were swarming to the urine and feeding on it.

When they tested the dog's urine, they found sugar in it—a sure sign of diabetes. The dog had been healthy before surgery, so they concluded that removing the pancreas had caused diabetes. This was the connection Johann Brunner had been unable to make in 1709.

After performing more tests, Minkowski and von Mering concluded that a healthy pancreas prevents diabetes by releasing a substance that controls the way sugar is used in the body. But they had no idea what that mysterious substance was. Over the next thirty years, scientists tried in vain to find it, and some even came close. During this time, patients with diabetes continued to be subjected to a variety of "cures," including opium, special diets, and bloodletting, which meant cutting the patient and allowing him to bleed for a specified period of time.

After Minkowski and von Mering's discovery, research focused on the pancreas as the source of diabetes. Remember Paul Langerhans, the German medical student who discovered "heaps of cells" in the pancreas?

## Pancreas: Home of a Million Islets

The pancreas is a flat, leaf-shaped gland located between the stomach and the spine. It has a double function. First, it is a digestive organ, making enzymes or chemicals that break down carbohydrates, fats, and proteins in the small intestine. And second, it is a hormone-producing organ. Hormones are chemicals that control the function of certain cells or organs.

Insulin is the main hormone produced by the pancreas. Insulin controls the amount of glycogen the liver stores, the amount of glucose the liver releases, and the amount of glucose that gets into the cells to be used as fuel.

The islets of Langerhans are groups of cells inside the pancreas that produce and release insulin and other hormones. About a million islet cells are contained in the 6-inch-long pancreas. Although five types of islet cells exist, beta cells are in the majority. Their job is to produce insulin and release just the right amount into the bloodstream to keep blood sugar levels steady all day long.

Unfortunately, beta cells get destroyed in type 1 diabetes. But there are so many, symptoms do not occur until 90 percent of them are damaged. This is when type 1 diabetes develops.

Islet of Langerhans cells are found in the pancreas. Beta cells, shown here, in orange, produce insulin.

In the early 1900s, after Langerhans's death, researchers began seriously investigating these islets (or islands) for clues to the cause of and cure for diabetes. In 1900, a young American researcher named Eugene Lindsay Opie discovered that deterioration of the islets of Langerhans in the pancreas led to diabetes. In 1916, Sir Edward Sharpey-Schafer, a London physician, theorized that the islets of Langerhans produced a substance that controlled how the body uses carbohydrates. He called this substance "insuline."

During this time, patients with diabetes continued to be subjected to a variety of "cures," including opium, special diets, and bloodletting.

Frederick Banting's experiments led to groundbreaking discoveries about the nature of diabetes. This painting shows him standing, with a seated assistant, possibly Charles Best.

Once these discoveries were made, a new experimental treatment emerged—feeding patients pieces of fresh pancreas or a liquid pancreas extract. However, these treatments failed. Researchers thought it was because the digestive enzymes in the pancreas were destroying the insulin. They needed to extract the insulin from the pancreas before it was destroyed. But how?

## THE DISCOVERY OF INSULIN

The biggest breakthrough in the history of diabetes occurred in 1922. Frederick Banting, a Canadian surgeon fresh out of medical school, had long been interested in diabetes. In 1920, he was struggling to earn a living as a doctor in private practice and for extra money he took a second job as a demonstrator in surgery and anatomy at Western University in London, Ontario, Canada. He had to give a lecture on the pancreas, so he did some research on the organ.

Talk about fate! During his research, he came across a newly published article by Dr. Moses Barron called "The Relation of the Islets of Langerhans to Diabetes." The article said that the pancreas shriveled if the pancreatic ducts were blocked, but the islets of Langerhans remained undamaged. It also said that as long as the islets were normal, diabetes did not develop, even with a shriveled pancreas.

The idea kept Banting awake that night. Could the islets hold the key to the mystery of diabetes? In the middle of the night, he scribbled the following note to himself: "Diabetus. Ligate pancreatic ducts of dogs. Keep dogs alive till acini degenerate leaving Islets. Try to isolate the internal secretion of these to relieve glycosurea."[4]

Banting planned to tie off the duct that connects the pancreas to the small intestine, destroying most of the pancreas so it would stop releasing digestive enzymes into the intestine. He hoped the islets of Langerhans would keep on working and that from them he would be able to extract the mysterious hormone that was the key to diabetes.

## Leonard Thompson: Insulin Pioneer

Fourteen-year-old Leonard Thompson was wasting away from diabetes. He had been diagnosed with the disease when he was 11, and over the years he became more and more ill. Finally, he became a patient at Toronto General Hospital. He was weak, bedridden, and weighed only 65 pounds. The doctors gave him only a few weeks to live.

LEONARD THOMPSON
First patient to receive insulin in
Toronto.

**Leonard Thompson's health greatly improved after he received the first insulin injections ever in 1922.**

A few miles away at the University of Toronto, Frederick Banting, Charles Best, and their team of researchers had just discovered a treatment for diabetes: a pancreatic extract they called insulin. They needed a patient to test it on, and Leonard was the perfect candidate.

But first, Banting and Best tested the insulin on themselves. Aside from soreness at the injection sites (places where the needle was inserted), the men had no unpleasant side effects. So they decided it was safe to give Leonard the insulin, and on January 11, 1922, he received his first insulin injection.

Leonard received injections of "thick brown muck" in each buttock, an accurate description of insulin in those days.[5] Although his blood sugar dropped temporarily, he developed infections at the injection sites and became even sicker. The researchers decided the insulin was not pure enough, so J.B. Collip, a biochemist on the team, quickly developed a purified extract. Leonard was given an injection of it on January 23. This time there were no side effects and it worked!

Within 24 hours, Leonard's blood sugar dropped from sky high to nearly normal and he improved from being barely conscious to alert and aware. With regular insulin injections, Leonard gained weight, recovered his energy, and was able to be discharged from the hospital. He continued with the insulin injections and lived a reasonably healthy life for another 13 years until he died of pneumonia in 1935.

Before he could conduct his experiments, Banting needed a laboratory. So he went to his alma mater, the University of Toronto, in search of laboratory space. In the summer of 1921, J. J. R. Macleod, head of the physiology department, gave Banting an unused lab on the top floor of the medical school and offered him the use of two assistants. One was Charles Best, who was about to enter medical school. Best is said to have won a coin toss with the other lab assistant to see which of them would work with Banting. Best had no idea that this unpaid job would lead to one of the greatest scientific discoveries in history and make him famous!

## THE EXPERIMENTS BEGIN

Banting and Best went to work. Banting performed the surgeries on the dogs' pancreases, giving them diabetes. Best measured urine and blood sugars and performed other lab tests. Meanwhile, they succeeded in removing the hormone from the islets of Langerhans of a group of healthy dogs. A few months later, they took this hormone and injected it into the dogs that had developed diabetes. The dogs' blood sugar levels went down and they got better! One dog, "Marjorie," stayed alive with pancreatic extract injections for 70 days. (Later, Banting and Best would discover that insulin could also be extracted from undamaged pancreases.)

During this time, Macleod realized groundbreaking work was being done and expanded the project, joining the research team himself and hiring more researchers. One obstacle was extracting enough of the hormone (which they first called *isletin* and then *insulin*, from the Latin word for "island") to continue the research; another was making sure the extract was pure enough. Macleod brought in biochemist J.B. Collip to work on purifying the extract. By the spring of 1921, the team came up with a form of insulin made from the pancreases of cattle from slaughterhouses. They believed it was pure enough to use on humans.

In January 1922, Leonard Thompson, age 14, became the first person to receive a successful insulin injection. And the rest, as they say, is history.

## EYES ON THE PRIZE

In early 1922, Banting and Best published a paper in a medical journal describing their discovery. News of the miracle drug insulin began spreading across the world. By 1923, pharmaceutical companies were mass producing insulin made from the pancreases of cattle and pigs. Countless lives were saved.

Banting, Best, Macleod, and Collip were hailed as heroes. But there was tension among the four researchers, who disagreed over whom should get the credit for the discovery. In 1923, the Nobel Prize for medicine and physiology was jointly awarded to Banting and Macleod. But Banting was furious, first threatening to refuse the prize and then publicly announcing that he would share his half of the award money with Best. Macleod then agreed to split his prize money with Collip.

Historians have written several versions of this story. It is possible that Banting's generosity with the prize money had more to do with his anger at Macleod than his gratitude for the work Best had done. One story says that Banting felt Macleod's main contribution was providing laboratory space, not helping with the research. Another story says that Collip tried to hide the formula for purifying insulin so he could patent the drug himself and that he and Banting had a fist fight over this issue. A political cartoon (now lost) supposedly showed Banting sitting on Collip and choking him, with the caption underneath reading, "The Discovery of Insulin."[6]

After work, the researchers may not have been best friends. But during work hours, they toiled together to make one of the most important medical discoveries in history. They were young, and full of energy and idealism, with big dreams and egos to match. To this day, no other discovery in the field of diabetes research has come close to equaling the discovery of insulin.

## ADVANCES IN TREATMENT

Medical advances since the discovery of insulin have led to a much better understanding of diabetes as well as far better treatments for the disease. Once insulin hit the market, researchers temporarily stopped trying to find a cure for diabetes and concentrated on just controlling the disease. But by the 1930s, they realized that diabetes was more complicated than they originally thought and that more effective and easier-to-use treatments were needed.

> To this day, no other discovery in the field of diabetes research has come close to equaling the discovery of insulin.

In 1935, Roger Hinsworth discovered that two types of diabetes existed: "insulin sensitive" (called type 1 today) and "insulin insensitive" (called type 2 today). This discovery showed that diabetes is not caused by lack of insulin alone and paved the way for the new treatments described below.

### Improved Insulins

Starting in the late 1930s, several new types of cattle and pig insulin were developed to better control blood sugar levels. A longer-acting insulin called protamine

ANIMAL VS. HUMAN INSULIN

n the early days, insulin was made by grinding up pig and cow pancreases and purifying the mixture.

Although early insulins lowered blood sugar quickly, the body also used them up quickly. Their purity and strength were also questionable.

Eventually, longer-acting, purified animal insulins were developed, and they were used for many years. But with more and more people being diagnosed with diabetes, there was always a chance the supply would run low. In addition, although pig and cow insulin is very similar to insulin produced by the human body, some people were allergic to it. Their immune systems saw the insulin as a foreign substance and destroyed it.

Today, human insulin is used almost exclusively, but it is not made from human pancreases. It is produced by genetic engineering. The human insulin gene is put into rapidly multiplying bacteria, which triggers the bacteria to make insulin.

zinc insulin (PZI), developed in 1936, decreased the number of injections needed per day. Two other longer-acting insulins, neutral protamine Hagedorn (NPH) and lente, were created in the following years and are still used today.

In 1978, the first synthetic (man-made) insulin was developed, and in 1983, scientists made human insulin by genetically altering bacteria. In 1996, human insulin analogs were created. Analogs are genetically altered insulins that produce a certain effect; for example, better glucose control after meals. They are most helpful in patients who have trouble controlling their diabetes. Human lispro is a fast-acting insulin analog that can be taken in 15 minutes or less before meals.

## Diabetes Pills

In the 1950s, the first pill was developed to treat type 2 diabetes. These drugs, called sulfonyureas, stimulated the islet cells in the pancreas to produce insulin. In 1995, the drug metformin was approved for use in the United States. Metformin is usually used as first-line therapy by itself, and can be combined with any other drug for diabetes, including insulin. It makes the body more sensitive to insulin and increases the ability of the muscles to use insulin. Another drug, acarbose, delays carbohydrate digestion by keeping glucose levels from rising suddenly after meals. Today, there are six types of oral drugs to treat type 2 diabetes, two non-insulin injectable drugs, and many different types of insulin.

## Better Testing Methods

In the 1960s, urine strips were invented and testing blood sugar levels became much easier. People simply urinated on the test strip and checked its color. If the strip turned blue, there was no sugar in their urine; if it turned orange, sugar was present. Before urine strips, people had to use a complicated method involving test tubes.

In 1986, blood glucose meters were approved for home use and eventually replaced urine testing for most patients. Patients prick their fingers and then test a droplet of blood for glucose by placing it on a test strip and inserting the strip into the meter. Some meters can measure blood glucose in as little as five seconds. Meters also give a more accurate measurement than urine testing and can record very low glucose levels that urine testing cannot.

## Some meters can measure blood glucose in as little as five seconds.

### Easier Ways to Take Insulin

Other advances in the 1960s included the single-use, disposable syringe and needle. Old needles were large and became dull, so they had to be sharpened with pumice stones. Besides being less painful, the new needles were more convenient because they were disposable. Reusing needles meant sterilizing them by boiling for 20 minutes before each use.

The first insulin pump was designed in the late 1970s. These pumps dispense insulin continuously through a small needle inserted into the skin so injections are not necessary. The first pumps were large and had to be carried in a backpack. Today's pumps are small, inconspicuous, and can be carried in a pocket or clipped to a belt.[7]

## Transplants

During the last 50 years, doctors have learned to transplant both the pancreas and just the islet cells. These operations may be the only hope for people with type 1 diabetes who cannot control their glucose levels even with frequent insulin injections or an insulin pump.

The first pancreas transplant was performed in 1966 at the University of Minnesota. The patient's blood glucose levels improved but she died three months later. Today, the procedure has been developed and improved; more than 1,000 pancreas transplants are done every year in the United States.

In 1974, the first islet cell transplant was performed, also at the University of Minnesota. Unfortunately, the patient died shortly afterward. In 2000, doctors at the University of Alberta in Edmonton, Canada, introduced a procedure that involves injecting islet cells from deceased donors into a blood vessel in the patient's abdomen. The cells then travel to the pancreas and start producing insulin. Several hundred islet cell transplants have been done so far using the Edmond Protocol.[8]

Thirty-five hundred years have passed since the ancient Egyptians wrote about a disease marked by excessive urination. Learning about diabetes and discovering insulin has been a long and difficult process that is still not over. Many more discoveries are waiting to be made in the twenty-first century. Now more than ever, scientists are focused on a cure for this disease that, in many ways, still remains a mystery.

# CHAPTER FOUR

# Preventing Diabetes

**B**en Franklin once said, "An ounce of prevention is worth a pound of cure." This is undoubtedly the case when it comes to type 2 diabetes. Type 1 diabetes, on the other hand, cannot be prevented, and cures for both types remain stubbornly out of reach. But ongoing research is uncovering more and more about diabetes, its causes, and steps that everyone can take to prevent this disease.

Unfortunately, diabetes has already affected 246 million people worldwide, and the numbers continue to grow.[1] In the United States alone, an estimated 20.8 million people, or 7 percent of the population, have diabetes. About 154,000 of these are children and teens.[2]

A healthy diet can help prevent diabetes or treat it once it develops.

In the United States alone, an estimated 20.8 million people, or 7 percent of the population, have diabetes.

Our schools, families, and even the media provide Americans with important health information; nevertheless, many people remain uninformed about the causes, treatments, and especially the preventive measures for diabetes.

## WHY IS DIABETES ON THE RISE?

Much information is available about the dramatic increase in rates of type 2 diabetes and about the appearance of the disease in young people the last 25 years. In the past, type 2 diabetes occurred mostly in middle-aged and older adults who were inclined to exercise less and who lost muscle mass and gained weight as a result. In fact, being older than age 45 is a known risk factor for type 2 diabetes. But today, many kids spend hours in front of the TV and computer daily, and their diets are growing less and less healthy. Consequently, 17 percent of American children and teens are overweight—three times as many as in 1980—which makes them prone to type 2 diabetes.[3]

Indeed, maintaining a healthy weight and engaging in daily physical activity are critical in preventing type 2 diabetes, and today, many people of all ages are gaining weight and not exercising enough—two major risk factors for this type of the disease.[4]

## A Weighty Problem

About 80 percent of people with type 2 diabetes are either overweight or obese.[5] Studies show that having an "apple" shape, with too much fat around the waist, makes people more prone to type 2 diabetes than having a "pear" shape, with excess fat below the waist. People become overweight because they take in more calories than their body needs. Even healthy, nutritious food is stored as fat if a person eats too much of it. The more extra calories one consumes, the more existing fat cells stretch. Brand new fat cells may grow.

The more fat cells a person has, the more his cells resist insulin. Whenever a person eats, blood sugar levels rise, alerting the beta cells in the pancreas to produce insulin. But when a person continually overeats, his beta cells are on constant alert and become overtaxed. Eventually, these cells become damaged or wear out and type 2 diabetes results.

## The Exercise Issue

Everyone knows that physical activity burns calories and helps people lose weight or maintain a healthy weight. An active body also requires glucose for energy, so less glucose accumulates in the blood of a person who exercises frequently. Physical activity also builds muscle, and muscle cells attract and burn glucose. In short, exercise makes you a lean, mean, glucose-burning machine! By sitting around instead of moving around, people end up with less muscle tissue to consume glucose and thereby more glucose in their bloodstreams. This can make them prone to type 2 diabetes.

## cool ideas

### Counting Your Steps

Not motivated to exercise? Wearing a pedometer can help get you moving. These inexpensive gadgets can be clipped to a person's waistband to sense the body's motion and record the number of steps taken and the distance traveled. Some people use pedometers only when they take a walk. Others put them on as soon as they get dressed in the morning to keep track of how many steps they take throughout the day. Exercise gurus recommend 6,000 steps a day for health and 10,000 for weight loss. So clip it on and get going!

## PREVENTING TYPE 2 DIABETES

Type 2 diabetes can often be prevented or delayed by eating right, maintaining a healthy weight, and getting plenty of exercise.

How do we know this? Through research studies. For example, a three-year study called the Diabetes Prevention Program examined the role of a healthy diet and exercise in preventing type 2 diabetes. All 3,234 subjects had a good chance of developing diabetes because they were overweight, they already had impaired glucose tolerance (prediabetes), and almost half of them were from racial and ethnic backgrounds that are more prone to type 2 diabetes than others.

The subjects were divided into three groups. The first group went on a low-fat diet and exercised 30 minutes a day, five days a week; the second group took a diabetes pill called metformin; and the third group took placebo pills instead of metformin. Although the second and third groups were given advice on diet and exercise, they were not required to follow the advice.

The results were striking: People in the diet and exercise group each lost 10 to 20 pounds and lowered their risk of getting diabetes by 58 percent. Those aged 60 and older reduced their risk of developing the disease by 71 percent. Put another way, only 5 percent of the diet and exercise group developed diabetes each year during the study compared to 11 percent in the other groups.

The conclusion? The diet/exercise combo keeps weight steady in normal-weight people and causes weight loss in overweight people. Healthy eating habits and exercise reduce the risk of type 2 diabetes by helping the body use insulin and convert glucose to energy.[6]

### Components of a Healthful Diet

We have established that healthy eating is an important component of diabetes prevention. But what exactly does a healthy diet entail? Most people have seen the food pyramid developed by the USDA. The pyramid has changed over the years as research has uncovered new facts about food's relationship to certain diseases. In 2005, the USDA updated the pyramid and added an interactive online tool at www.mypyramid.gov. People can actually type in their age, weight, height, and how much they exercise and the Web site will generate personalized suggestions on how to improve their health habits.

The USDA recommends a diet high in fruits, vegetables, whole grains, lean meat, fish, eggs, beans,

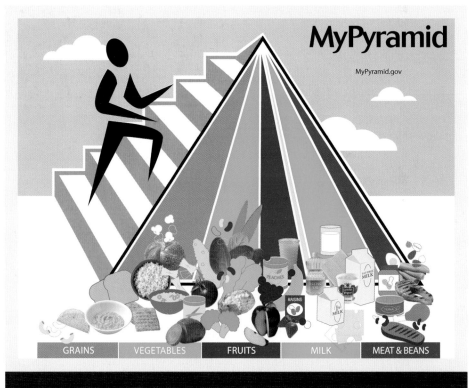

**MyPyramid**

MyPyramid.gov

| GRAINS | VEGETABLES | FRUITS | MILK | MEAT & BEANS |

In 2005, the USDA unveiled a new food pyramid (above) to replace the one used since 1992. The new pyramid also includes exercise recommendations.

## Dig Into Dairy

Consuming low-fat dairy foods, such as yogurt, cottage cheese, and skim or 1 percent milk, may help prevent type 2 diabetes. Two studies—one of 37,000 women and the other of 84,000 women—found that those who ate the most dairy products decreased their risk of getting type 2 diabetes by one-fifth and one-third, respectively. Researchers are investigating whether dairy products affect men the same way. But nutritionists agree that eating two to three servings of dairy products a day is a healthy choice.[7]

Recent studies suggest that low-fat dairy foods may help prevent diabetes and other health problems.

nuts, and low-fat dairy products, and low in added salt, sugar, and saturated fats. This means avoiding junk food (such as chips), fried foods (such as French fries), sugary food (such as regular soda) or desserts (such as cakes, pies, and donuts), and just about anything from a fast food restaurant except a salad with low-fat dressing. "Avoiding" means not making a habit of eating these foods, not banishing them from your life forever. Following the USDA's recommendations will help people maintain a healthy weight and live a healthy lifestyle.

Another reason to eat fruits, veggies, and whole grain breads and cereals is that they are high in insoluble (indigestible) fiber. This may make the body more sensitive to insulin so it moves from the bloodstream to the cells more efficiently. For those who need extra fiber, insoluble fiber supplements (pills and powders) are also readily available without prescription at the drugstore.

For grains (orange part of the pyramid), the USDA recommends that Americans eat at least three ounces of whole grain bread, cereal, crackers, rice, or pasta everyday. They recommend that at least half of the grains eaten every day be whole grains, not processed grains such as white flour or white rice.

The amount of vegetables (green part of the pyramid) recommended depends on a person's age and weight. Vegetables are important sources of vitamins, minerals, and fiber. Children eight years and older should eat at least two cups of vegetables a day; adult men at least three cups. Many Americans need to make better, more varied choices from this group and include lots of green, red, and leafy vegetables. Potatoes are a vegetable, for example, but no one vegetable should make up the bulk of a person's vegetable consumption.

Fruit (red part of the pyramid) consumption also depends on age, weight, and physical activity. People eight and over should consume at least 1½ cups of fruit every day, of many different kinds. Citrus fruits are rich in vitamin C; other fruits are rich in vitamin A.

Oils (yellow part of the pyramid) are full of fat calories, but they are vital for good cardiovascular, nervous system, and digestive health. Most Americans consume enough oil in the foods they eat. A person's allowance for oils depends on age, gender, and level of physical activity. Children over the age of eight and adults should consume no more than five to six teaspoons of oils a day.

Dairy (blue part of the pyramid) products, including milk, yogurt, and cheese, provide calcium and other important nutrients, but they can be calorie-laden and full of fat. Some people are lactose-intolerant and can't tolerate milk at all. For those who can, the USDA recommends consuming at least 3 cups of milk products a day for those eight and older. The USDA recommends low-fat and fat-free choices whenever possible.

Meat and beans (purple part of the pyramid) are full of protein. Meat includes fish, chicken, beef, pork, and other animals. The amount of food recommended from this group depends on age, gender, and level of physical activity. Most Americans eat enough from this group, but need to make leaner and more varied selections. The USDA recommends including vegetable sources of protein such as beans and peas and choosing lean, low-fat meats and poultry. Children older than eight and adults need between 5 and 6½ ounces a day.

### The Next Step

Being overweight is the main cause of type 2 diabetes. Eating right is one way to control weight; exercising is the other. Overweight people who lose just 7 to 10 percent of their current weight can cut their risk of getting type 2 diabetes in half.[8]

ng Diabetes

Working the muscles through exercise helps them use insulin and absorb glucose. But long sessions at the health club are not necessary. As little as 30 minutes of brisk walking five times a week can help prevent or reduce the risk of getting type 2 diabetes. In fact, any kind of exercise is beneficial. Mow the lawn, rake leaves, vacuum the house, ride a bike, shoot some hoops, or play Frisbee with the dog. Just keep moving!

From going for a jog to mowing the lawn, all kinds of exercise are good for the body.

### Another Preventive Measure

More than one study has linked smoking to type 2 diabetes. In a Harvard study of 85,000 female nurses, for instance, smoking was found to increase the risk of developing the disease. In another study of more than 21,000 male doctors, smokers of 20 or more cigarettes a day were 70 percent more likely to get type 2 diabetes than nonsmokers. Smoking is bad for your health, period.[9]

# Smoking is bad for your health, period.

### The Role of Heredity

One risk factor for diabetes cannot be changed—a person's genes. In one study of 200 adults with type 2

## What Is a Clinical Trial?

Clinical trials are studies that check the effectiveness and safety of new medicines or medical devices by testing them on large groups of people. These studies are often conducted by the federal government or large medical centers. Many people with incurable or hard-to-treat diseases want to take part in clinical trials because the trials offer the chance to try promising new treatments.

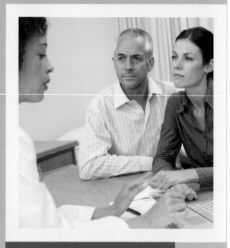

Subjects are usually divided into two groups: a group taking the new drug and a control group taking a placebo, an inactive substance that has no effect. People are not told whether they have been administered the real drug or the placebo. This way, researchers can see how effective a new drug is compared to taking no drug at all. Sometimes, the group taking the placebo sees improvement just from the power of suggestion!

**Clinical trials can help researchers learn how effective a new drug is.**

diabetes, about two-thirds had at least one close diabetic relative and nearly half had two close relatives with the disease.[10]

Each cell has 25,000 to 35,000 genes, chemicals that determine a person's outward traits, such as straight hair or blue eyes, and inward traits, such as a tendency to have diabetes. These traits are passed from generation to generation.

Studying certain ethnic groups reinforces the role that genes play in type 2 diabetes. Compared to white Americans of European descent, the following races and ethnic groups have higher rates of type 2 diabetes: African Americans, Asian Americans, Hispanic Americans (except Cuban Americans), Pacific Islanders, and Native Americans. American Indians have the highest rate of type 2 diabetes in the world. Gestational diabetes is also more common in many of these groups.[11]

## PREVENTING TYPE 1 DIABETES

So far, there is no way to prevent type 1 diabetes, which usually occurs in people under age 20. Researchers have experimented with vitamin supplements, drugs to suppress the immune system, low-dose insulin injections, and antibodies to keep the immune system from destroying beta cells in the pancreas. Research is ongoing, and some of these methods show promise.

Researchers *have* managed to pinpoint who is susceptible to type 1 diabetes. Unfortunately, the only proven risk factor—heredity—is out of a person's control.

The SEARCH for Diabetes in Youth project studied 6,000 children and adolescents with diabetes from

## What Is Gestational Diabetes?

Gestation is another word for pregnancy. During pregnancy, some women who did not have diabetes previously develop the disease. This usually goes away after the baby is born, but unfortunately, glucose levels do not return to normal in 5 to 10 percent of women. These women are then classified as type 2 diabetics after they give birth. Another 20 to 50 percent of women with gestational diabetes will develop type 2 diabetes within 5 to 10 years of giving birth.

Why does gestational diabetes occur? One theory is that hormones normally produced during pregnancy block insulin's action. Another theory is that a woman might have diabetes before pregnancy and not realize it; then the weight gain and hormonal changes stress her body and reveal the diabetes. A third theory is that obesity is the trigger, since gestational diabetes is more common in women who are overweight. So being at a healthy weight before pregnancy might help prevent this type of diabetes.[13]

2000 to 2005 and found that 56 percent of those with type 1 diabetes had a parent, sibling, or grandparent with the disease. This study reinforced what has been known for years: that a person's genes make him vulnerable to type 1 diabetes. On the other hand, 44 percent of type 1 diabetics in the study did not share the disease with a close family member. So heredity is not always a factor.[12]

The SEARCH project also found something surprising: Many of the young people with type 1 diabetes were overweight. Obesity is a known risk factor for type 2 diabetes. But these recent findings have researchers wondering: Could being overweight speed up or encourage the development of type 1 diabetes, too? More studies need to be done before obesity can definitely be linked to type 1 diabetes. But experts agree that maintaining a desirable weight is an important part of a healthy lifestyle, whether a person has diabetes or not.[14]

There are several other theories about the causes of and preventive measures for type 1 diabetes. They range from catching a mysterious virus, to eating certain foods (such as cow's milk as an infant), to not getting enough vitamin D. But none of these theories has been proven.

Most likely, type 1 diabetes is caused by a combination of factors. For example, someone might start with a genetic predisposition and then be exposed to a virus, leading to type 1 diabetes. In the future, more risk factors will be identified, and doctors will be able to better advise their patients on preventing type 1 diabetes.

For now, people whose close relatives have type 1 diabetes can determine their risk of developing the disease by having a blood test. The more insulin antibodies in their blood, the higher the chance of someday developing type 1 diabetes.

how real teens deal

## Tesch: Inspired by Diabetes

Tesch West, age 16, loves to talk about diabetes and share her experiences. As the 2007–2008 National Youth Advocate for the American Diabetes Association (ADA), she gives radio and television interviews, attends conferences, and speaks in front of hundreds of people. She helped organize America's Walk for Diabetes in her hometown of Salt Lake City, Utah, and visits diabetes camps to encourage other young people with the disease.

But Tesch was not always so confident and poised. Six years ago, when she was diagnosed with type 1 diabetes, she was just as confused and scared as any other 10-year-old would be. She had been listless and using the bathroom a lot, so her mom took her to the emergency room, where her blood was drawn and tested. Normal blood sugar is under 100 mg/dl and Tesch's was 836!

Tesch remembered: "I didn't know what diabetes was. My mom was really scared, too. I had to stay in the hospital three days, and that's when I realized how big this was. I asked my mom, 'Why me?'"[15]

That was the first and last time she ever asked that question. "All of the experiences I've had make up for the cost [of having diabetes]. I wouldn't change it," she said.[16]

That remark is pretty amazing, but Tesch is known for her optimism. In her hospital bed, she began to learn all she could about diabetes. The doctor said she was the only kid who ever took notes. Her transition back to fifth grade was smooth, too, because her teacher also had diabetes and helped Tesch recognize when her blood sugar was fluctuating. Before long, Tesch was giving her teacher pointers on how to count carbohydrates!

Tesch got an insulin pump in sixth grade and said it works well with her hectic schedule. She cannot always eat at set times, but the pump allows her to skip meals occasionally because it can be programmed to give more or less insulin depending on how much (or how little) she eats.

People are often curious about the pump, but Tesch does not mind answering questions—one of her goals is raising diabetes awareness. She said her close friends are "really savvy" about the signs of low blood sugar and watch out for her. They also understand if she does not want to eat at fast food restaurants. "Now that I know the carb value, fat, and calories, I'm a lot more cautious about what I eat," Tesch said. "It's hard to eat candy bars."[17]

As a tenth grader, Tesch's favorite subject was human biology, but her work as a diabetes advocate has also gotten her interested in politics. "I'd like to combine medicine and politics, or maybe work as a lobbyist for the ADA on Capitol Hill," she said.[18]

What advice does she have for teens who have just been diagnosed with diabetes? "It gets better. The more you learn, the less scary it is," she said. "Diabetes won't impede any of your goals or dreams, maybe it's even inspirational. Get involved in your community, volunteer. My mom says the best way to get your mind off yourself is to help someone else."[19]

For Tesch West, diabetes is not an obstacle—it's an inspiration.

# CHAPTER FIVE

# Testing and Treatment

Before people realize they have diabetes, their bodies send out warning signals. They feel hungry and thirsty all the time. They keep waking up at night to go to the bathroom. They feel weak and lethargic. Sometimes, their vision is blurry. These symptoms are frightening, but they can be a blessing in disguise because they make people realize they need to see a doctor right away.

Symptoms often occur suddenly in individuals with type 1 diabetes, which usually affects young people. A child or teen feels fine one day, and then feels very sick the next, prompting parents to call the doctor. On the other hand, people with type 2 diabetes, which usually affects adults, may not notice the symptoms because they often occur gradually. Many people with type 2 diabetes discover they

Willingness to learn about symptoms and treatment can help people to successfully manage their diabetes.

have high glucose levels by accident, when they go for a routine examination and their doctor says the results of a blood test suggest they may have the disease.

Eventually, people with undiagnosed type 2 diabetes have increased thirst, frequent urination, and other classic symptoms of this disease. If they wait too long to visit their doctors after these symptoms appear, they can develop serious problems with their eyes, heart, and other organs.

Thankfully, both type 1 and type 2 diabetes can be managed successfully. Once someone is diagnosed, treatment starts immediately. The doctor will prescribe a treatment plan and offer advice and guidance; he or she will also tell the patient to schedule regular office visits. But people with diabetes must learn all they can about the disease and take charge of their own treatment if they want to stay healthy.

Young children with type 1 will need their parents' help, but by the time they reach their early teens, most young people are experts at managing their diabetes. In fact, they usually know more about good nutrition and how their bodies work than their peers without diabetes. But getting to this point takes time and effort.

## TESTING, TESTING

What happens when a person goes to the doctor with symptoms of diabetes? First, the doctor will take a patient history. The doctor will ask exactly what symptoms have been experienced and will want to know if any family members have type 1 or type 2 diabetes. Physicians often ask about the patient's ethnic background, since certain ethnic groups have a higher risk of developing diabetes.

If the patient is a child, the doctor will ask the parents to help answer these questions.

Next, the doctor will conduct a physical examination, listening to the patient's heart and taking his temperature, pulse, and blood pressure, among other things. The doctor will also check the eyes, ears, nose, mouth, and throat, and assess the patient's general appearance to determine if he looks sick or well.

If the patient's history and physical examination suggest diabetes, the doctor will order blood tests to see if the patient's glucose level is high. Before blood tests were developed, urine testing was the only way to identify this problem, but this method is very inaccurate, so doctors no longer recommend it.

Today, a few different tests are used to measure the amount of glucose in the blood. They all involve inserting a needle into an arm vein, drawing out a small amount of blood, and then sending it to a laboratory. Some tests require the patient to fast—not eat or drink anything but water—for at least eight hours beforehand.

### Random Plasma Glucose Test

The random plasma glucose test measures the amount of glucose in the blood at any time of day. No fasting is required. This is one of several blood tests doctors order during a routine physical examination, and it is through this test that many individuals first find out they have type 2 diabetes. If the patient's blood glucose is higher than 200 mg/dl, the doctor will suspect diabetes and order a fasting plasma glucose test to be sure.[1]

# Hemoglobin A1C Test

This test does not diagnose diabetes. Rather, it assesses how well people are controlling their blood glucose by giving an average reading over time. This test is performed on diabetics about every three months in a lab or doctor's office and involves taking blood from an arm or finger. Fasting is not necessary.

What does hemoglobin have to do with controlling blood glucose? Hemoglobin is a protein inside red blood cells that transports oxygen and gives blood its red color. Glucose normally attaches itself to hemoglobin, thereby creating a molecule called HbA1C, or simply, A1C. When large quantities of glucose accumulate in the blood, much of it attaches to hemoglobin, causing A1C levels to rise.

The Hemoglobin A1C test works because red blood cells "remember" what happened between glucose and hemoglobin for two or three months. This is possible because glucose stays in the red blood cells for their whole lifespan, about 120 days. As old cells die and new ones replace them, the hemoglobin keeps a record of a person's A1C over time, and this record can be viewed under a microscope. The American Diabetes Association recommends keeping the A1C level under 7, which means that glucose is attached to 7 percent of the hemoglobin molecules. This test is not meant to replace regular home glucose monitoring, and people with diabetes still need to check their blood glucose levels several times a day.

### Fasting Plasma Glucose Test

A fasting plasma glucose test is the preferred test for diagnosing diabetes in children, men, and women who are not pregnant. The patient must fast for at least eight hours, so the test is usually performed first thing in the morning. Remember that eating causes one's blood glucose level to rise. But in untreated diabetes, extra glucose remains in the blood, even when no food has been consumed. This causes high readings on the fasting plasma glucose test. A normal fasting blood glucose level is less than 100 mg/dl. A reading of 100 to 125 mg/dl indicates prediabetes, which means a person has a good chance of developing type 2 diabetes. If the reading is 126 or higher, diabetes is the anticipated diagnosis, but to confirm, the test is repeated on a different day, and the reading must be 126 or higher both times.[2]

If a patient is under age 20 and his illness came on suddenly, he probably has type 1 diabetes; if he is older and obese, he probably has type 2 diabetes.

### Oral Glucose Tolerance Test

Sometimes the fasting plasma glucose test results are normal even when a patient has many symptoms of diabetes. When this happens, the doctor orders the more complicated oral glucose tolerance test. This test is especially useful for diagnosing prediabetes and is regularly used to diagnose gestational diabetes. It is performed at the doctor's office or a laboratory and involves taking blood samples at different times after the patient drinks a glucose solution, a mixture of glucose and water.

Pregnant women do not need to prepare for this test, but other patients must eat a balanced diet with 150 to 300 grams of car-bohydrates per day for three days before the test. During the eight hours prior to testing, they must not eat or drink any-thing besides water, must not smoke, and must not exercise strenuously.

Normal glu-cose levels are less than 140 mg/dl two hours after drink-ing the glucose solution. A level be-tween 140 and 199 mg/dl signals prediabetes, and a level of 200 mg/dl or over signals diabetes. Gestational diabetes is diagnosed if at least two blood glucose readings are above normal.[3]

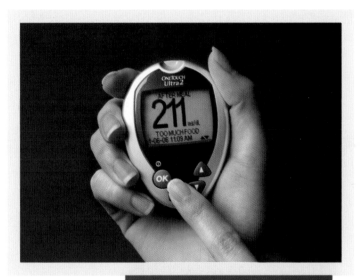

Blood glucose monitors are among the devices used to check glucose levels.

### Diagnosis

If tests reveal a high amount of glucose in the blood, the doctor will diagnose type 1 or type 2 diabetes based on the patient's family history, symptoms, additional tests, and physical characteristics. For example, if the patient is under age 20 and his illness came on suddenly, he probably has type 1 diabetes; if he is older and obese, he probably has type 2 diabetes. If the patient is pregnant, the diagnosis will be gestational diabetes.

## TREATING DIABETES

Whether a person has type 1 or type 2 diabetes, the goal is to control blood glucose so the patient will feel good, will be able to stay active, and will not experience complications later in life. The doctor will personalize a treatment plan according to the patient's age, weight, current health, and other factors. But all people need a combination of the following tools to manage their diabetes:

- Insulin and/or diabetes pills
- A device to check their glucose levels
- Regular exercise
- Healthy eating habits
- The willingness to take charge of one's own health
- Medical checkups

## INSULIN: THE FIRST LINE OF DEFENSE

Diabetes is caused by the lack of insulin in the body or resistance to insulin, so it is easy to understand why the primary treatment for type 1 diabetes involves replacing insulin. So far, no one has invented a pill that effectively replaces insulin itself, so everyone with type 1 diabetes and some people with type 2 diabetes have to inject insulin with a needle. Besides individual shots, insulin can also be administered with an insulin pump, but this, too, requires inserting a needle under the skin. People who inject insulin usually need several shots a day to maintain a healthy blood glucose level. Parents of young children with type 1 diabetes give them shots, but older children usually learn to do it themselves. No one likes shots, but eventually diabetics view shots the same way they do flossing their teeth—something that is necessary for good health that should be done efficiently so they can move on to more interesting things.

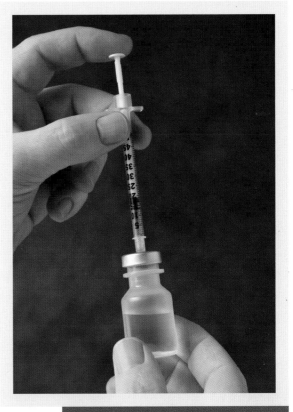

Shots of insulin help people with type 1 diabetes to maintain a healthy blood glucose level.

Why does insulin need to be administered so often? The purpose is to imitate the way a healthy pancreas works in people without diabetes. When a non-diabetic eats, just enough insulin is released from the pancreas to clear the glucose from the blood. In people with diabetes, giving precisely measured insulin at specific intervals can replicate this chain of events so glucose levels remain normal.

Insulin is usually injected into the abdomen, but the thighs, buttocks, backs of the arms, and other sites are also used. The injection must be made into a layer of fat just under the skin, above the muscle tissue, because injecting into a muscle hurts more and causes the insulin to be absorbed too quickly. People also need to rotate sites; that is, they must not inject into exactly the same spot every time they administer insulin. Because different body areas absorb insulin at different rates, the American Diabetes Association (ADA) advises injecting into different spots in the same general area to avoid large variations in blood glucose levels.

## TYPES OF INSULIN

Different types of insulin are used at different times of the day. Short-acting and rapid-acting insulins are injected before meals because they reach the bloodstream quickly. Intermediate-acting and long-acting insulins take longer to work, but they stay in the bloodstream longer so they are used before bed to control glucose over long periods of time.

## INJECTION DEVICES

There are three common ways to inject insulin: with a needle and syringe, with an insulin pen, or with an insulin pump.

## INSULIN PENS

Insulin pens are convenient and simple to use. Pressing the plunger delivers a precise dose of insulin.

Anyone who has ever had a shot knows what a needle and syringe look like. Today's syringes have very thin, disposable needles that are easy to use and hardly painful. Most people use this method to inject their insulin.

Insulin pens are the same size as regular pens so they are handy to carry. They are a combination insulin container and a syringe and come in two types: reusable and prefilled. Both types require specifying, or dialing in, the insulin dose and pressing the plunger, a button on the top of the pen, to give the injection.

Insulin pumps are computerized devices about the size of a cell phone that are attached to a belt or kept in a pocket. The pump has a tube with a small needle on the

## INSULIN PUMPS

About the size of a cell phone, an insulin pump is worn on a belt or kept in a pocket. A tube from the pump is attached to a needle that is inserted in the thigh or stomach to deliver a steady trickle of insulin 24 hours a day.

end, which is usually inserted under the skin of the thigh or stomach. The wearer programs the pump to deliver a steady trickle of insulin throughout the day, or can change the setting and press a button to deliver extra insulin at meals or other times when blood sugar levels get high.

Insulin pumps are mainly used by people with type 1 diabetes. They are convenient, but they must be watched carefully to make sure they do not malfunction or leak and cause blood glucose levels to plummet.

## DIABETES PILLS

Although there are no pills to replace insulin in type 1 diabetes, people with type 2 diabetes can take medicine to help control their blood glucose levels. They are usually prescribed when diet and exercise alone are not sufficient to manage a patient's type 2 diabetes.

There are six types of oral medications for type 2 diabetes. They each work in a different way to lower blood glucose. Some people find that a combination of two drugs works best. Usually, insulin is only prescribed to people with type 2 diabetes if all other methods fail. However, some studies have shown that the use of insulin shortly after type 2 diabetes is diagnosed, along with oral drugs, is the most effective course of treatment.[4]

## GLUCOSE MONITORING DEVICES

Glucose levels that are too high or too low can cause serious complications, so it is critical that people with diabetes check their glucose levels throughout the day. Everyday events that most people take for granted can make glucose levels fluctuate. For example, eating prompts blood glucose to rise, as does experiencing stress or having the flu. Glucose levels decrease when a person exercises or administers insulin or an oral diabetes drug.

# Everyday events that most people take for granted can make glucose levels fluctuate.

A blood glucose meter is the key to self-monitoring one's blood sugar levels. Today's digital meters measure the glucose contained in a single drop of blood, which is obtained from pricking the finger with a sharp but almost

## Testing Blood Glucose at Home

Almost all diabetics need to test their blood sugar at least once a day. They can do this at home or on the road with convenient, portable test kits that allow people to check their blood glucose levels whenever and wherever they want. These kits are available at drugstores and include a glucose meter, a lancing device, and test strips. Glucose meters are about the size of a cell phone and can display results on a screen in as little as five seconds. A lancing device is a finger-sized instrument with a small, pointed, disposable knife, or lancet, that punctures the skin, usually on a fingertip, to draw a drop of blood. Test strips are small, thin, disposable pieces of plastic coated with chemicals that react with glucose. To test glucose, people clean the puncture site with soap and water or alcohol and then follow these steps:

- Prick their fingertip with the lancet.
- Hold their finger down and gently squeeze the tip until a round drop of blood appears.
- Catch the drop on a test strip.
- Insert the test strip into the glucose meter according to the instructions in the user's manual.
- Read the test result (in mg/dl) on the display screen and record it in a logbook.

Some glucose meters work by measuring the amount of electricity passing through the test strip. Others measure how much light reflects from the test strip. Some new meters allow blood to be taken from the upper arm, thigh, or other parts of the body. Audio meters read the results aloud instead of displaying them.

painless instrument called a lancet. Blood is placed on a small test strip and then inserted into the meter. A digital readout appears on the screen in only a few seconds.

Today's blood glucose meters require only a single drop of blood and show results in just a few seconds.

The ADA advises adults with diabetes to achieve blood glucose levels between 90 and 130 mg/dl before meals and under 180 mg/dl at other times. This is called tight glucose control, and studies show that keeping blood glucose as close to the above numbers as possible dramatically reduces the risk of complications later in life.

Doctors recommend that people with type 1 diabetes check their glucose levels several times during the day. People with type 2 diabetes may only need to do this once a day. A logbook can help people keep track of when they tested and what the results were.

Eventually diabetics will also learn to engage in a more comprehensive type of self-monitoring, which goes beyond blood glucose testing with a digital meter. True self-monitoring takes practice, but with their doctor's help, people begin to understand exactly what affects their personal glucose levels and how much insulin, medicine, exercise, or food they require to counteract glucose ups and downs.

## THE EXERCISE ADVANTAGE

Everyone needs regular exercise. The Centers for Disease Control and Prevention recommends that adults get 30 minutes of moderate intensity exercise at least five days a week or 20 minutes of vigorous exercise at least three days a week. Children and adolescents should get at least 60 minutes of moderate intensity exercise every day.

Regular exercise helps people lose weight and handle stress. Exercise also prevents heart attacks, lowers cholesterol, and makes people feel and look better. But when diabetics exercise, they have to give it more thought than other people, because exercise affects blood glucose levels.

During exercise, cells, including those in the muscles, use glucose for energy. At the beginning of an exercise session the body burns stored glucose for fuel, but eventually, glucose supplies run low, so the muscles draw glucose from the blood. This causes blood glucose levels to drop, and some people with diabetes must take precautions to be sure levels do not drop too far or too fast. This can cause hypoglycemia, a medical emergency.

The problems associated with blood glucose levels and exercise are most common in people with type 1 diabetes. People with type 2 diabetes who are not taking insulin usually do not have swings in blood glucose levels that are large enough to be serious. But diabetics who use insulin must test their blood with a glucose meter before and after exercise and adjust their insulin to prevent dangerous drops in blood glucose. They may also need to have a small snack before exercising.

## What Is Hyperglycemia?

Hyperglycemia (high blood sugar) occurs when diabetics do not take enough insulin or other diabetes medication, or when they eat/drink too much carbohydrate or don't get enough exercise. When someone does not follow his treatment plan carefully, glucose levels stay high and, over time, the kidneys, blood vessels, teeth, gums, eyes, and nerves are damaged. The American Diabetes Association defines hyperglycemia as blood glucose levels above 130 mg/dl when fasting and above 180 mg/dl two hours after eating.

Hyperglycemia can also occur suddenly, even in people who are usually careful about managing their diabetes. Extremely high glucose levels create a medical emergency that can progress to shock, coma, and even death. Causes of severe hyperglycemia include missing an insulin dose, injecting insulin that has gone bad, or clogged insulin pump tubing.

Diabetic ketoacidosis (DKA) is different from severe hyperglycemia, although the two conditions can occur together. Severe hyperglycemia is usually present in DKA, but not always. Most hyperglycemia, even if the level is very high, won't cause DKA if enough insulin is around. DKA usually occurs due to missed insulin doses or an illness that increases the need for insulin.

DKA occurs in the following manner: When the body does not have enough insulin, the muscles break down fat for energy. The by-product of this breakdown is ketones, acidic products that accumulate in the blood and poison it. While this is happening, glucose spills into the urine, the kidneys make more urine, and the person becomes dehydrated. The toxic combination of ketones and dehydration is DKA.

*Continued on next page*

*Continued from previous page*

Diabetic ketoacidosis can happen without warning. Whenever a blood glucose reading is over 240 mg/dl or a person feels sick, he should check his urine for ketones with a urine test strip. These strips turn a certain color when urine touches them, and the result is read by placing the strip next to the color chart in the package.

Symptoms of DKA include stomach pains, vomiting, lack of appetite, fever with flushed or dry skin, weakness, sleepiness, blurred vision, trouble breathing, fruity breath odor, and typical signs of hyperglycemia (extreme thirst, dry mouth, and frequent urination). Anyone with ketones in their urine and some of these signs should call the doctor immediately. Treatment involves taking extra rapid- or short-acting insulin right away and drinking lots of fluids to prevent further dehydration. Diabetics should also warn friends and coworkers about the signs of DKA and tell them what to do should they suspect this condition.

People with type 2 diabetes can also have hyperglycemia episodes (or high blood sugar), although they do not usually have DKA or ketones in their urine. Blood glucose levels can rise as high as 1,000 mg/dl, often before type 2 diabetes is diagnosed. Coma can occur in severe cases.

Exercise also affects how insulin works in the body. Working out increases blood flow, so injected insulin works faster. Exercise also increases the muscles' and tissues' sensitivity to insulin, so people may be able to inject a little less insulin or eat a little more food and still maintain a healthy blood glucose level. People with type 2 diabetes who exercise regularly may even be able to stop taking insulin or other diabetes drugs.

## EATING RIGHT

There are a lot of mistaken beliefs about diabetes, most of which have to do with forbidden foods. Some people think that diabetics have to give up desserts for the rest of their lives and count every calorie down to the last pea on the plate. This is a misconception. People with diabetes should follow a healthy diet and eat a variety of foods, just like everyone else. But they do have to think carefully about what, how much, and when they eat.

This is especially critical for those who take insulin because they have to balance the amount of carbohydrates

---

DIABETES FOOD PYRAMID

The American Diabetes Association's food pyramid divides food into six groups. The largest group, and the base of the pyramid, contains breads, grains, and other starches. These are the foods the ADA recommends people with diabetes eat the most of. The smallest group, on the top, contains fats, oils, and sweets. These are the foods to eat very sparingly. However, in January 2008, the ADA issued the following statement: "For weight loss, either low-carbohydrate or fat-restricted diets may be effective in the short term (up to 1 year)."

---

they consume and the amount of insulin they inject. People with type 2 diabetes who do not use insulin need to eat a healthy, balanced diet, too, especially if they are overweight. Their goal is to eat healthier and lose weight so they will not develop complications in the future. Unfortunately, some patients with type 2 diabetes will not be able to stop their insulin therapy although they follow diet and exercise plans almost perfectly.

Some people think that diabetics have to give up desserts for the rest of their lives and count every calorie down to the last pea on the plate. This is a misconception.

At first, planning meals can be confusing and time consuming, but eventually, it becomes second nature. Families often find that everyone is eating better when there is a person with diabetes in the house.

## MEAL PLANNING AND PORTION SIZE

Nutrition guidelines for diabetics specify certain amounts of proteins, carbohydrates, and fats that are allowed each day, so food must be weighed and measured. Some people get so good at judging portion sizes that they do not always need to weigh and measure food. For example, they know that one serving of meat is the size of a deck of cards, and one serving of cooked pasta is the size of an ice cream scoop.

People can also plan meals using food exchanges. With food exchanges, food is divided into six exchange lists, similar to the food pyramid. People can trade one food on a particular list for another food on the same list; for example, a cup of oatmeal can be exchanged for two slices of bread because both foods equal one bread exchange.

Learning about portion sizes can make healthy eating easier.

A third meal planning method is counting carbohydrates. People with type 1 diabetes often do this because it gives them more flexibility in food choices. They add up all the carbohydrates they plan to eat at each meal so they know exactly how much insulin to inject before eating to handle the carbohydrates. Lists of carbohydrate counts can be found on the Internet, in books, and on food labels. Carbohydrate counting is not an excuse to eat junk food just because insulin can be injected to "cover" it. People on this plan still have to eat healthily. Otherwise, a person might develop a resistence to insulin from overuse, and this can lead to serious health problems.

## Brian: Diabetes Is No Excuse

Brian Hadley's* parents were worried. Their lively 7-year-old had suddenly become tired and cranky all the time. He could not get enough to drink and was visiting the bathroom six times a night. After a week of this behavior, Brian's parents took him to the doctor. The diagnosis caught then completely by surprise: type 1 diabetes.

"My blood sugar was over 600," Brian, now age 16, remembered (normal blood sugar is under 100 mg/dl). "If your blood sugar is high, you're not the happiest camper."[5]

The doctor sent Brian and his parents to the emergency room immediately. There, Brian received his first insulin shot. "I remember getting that first shot," he said. "I thought it was going to be a one-time thing. At first, I didn't want to get the shots, so I ran around the house trying to get away from my mom," Brian recalled.[6]

That was nine years ago. When he was in 4th grade, Brian began to administer his own shots; then in 6th grade he got an insulin pump, which delivers insulin automatically. Now a high school sophomore, he says programming the pump and counting carbohydrates is "like second nature." He said the pump does not cramp his style, even when he snowboards, rides dirt bikes, or wrestles on the school team. He said people often mistake the pump for an MP3 player.

But like many athletes, Brian has a very low percentage of body fat, which makes selecting an insertion site for his pump difficult. "The only place I have enough fat is my butt," he said.[7] Brian does not make a big deal out of this. Luckily, the needle only has to be changed every three days.

Brian plays sports and does everything else a teen without diabetes does – maybe even more. "Diabetes is no excuse for not trying something new," he said.[8]

* Not his real name.

## THE GLYCEMIC INDEX

The ADA has designed its own food pyramid, with carbohydrates on the bottom level. The organization recommends eating at least six servings of healthy carbohydrates (whole grains and fruits and vegetables) a day. Even though carbohydrates cause blood glucose to rise, they deliver essential vitamins, minerals, fiber, and energy.

The key is choosing carbohydrates with a low glycemic index (GI). The GI is a popular catchword in diet books, so popular that Googling it brings up 208,000 sites! Even so, most people are confused by this measure. In a nutshell, the GI ranks by number foods containing carbohydrates based on how they affect blood glucose levels. Foods that make levels increase the most and the fastest have the highest GI (70 or over). Examples are candy, regular soda, and white bread. Low GI foods (55 and below), such as whole grain breads and most fruits and vegetables, do not cause such a rapid increase in blood glucose levels. Obviously, people with diabetes should avoid high GI foods in favor of low GI foods, but they should never give up carbohydrates altogether.

## THE TRUTH ABOUT SUGAR

Sugar is not the villain we once thought it was. People with diabetes can indulge in an occasional piece of cake, as long as they adjust their insulin dose or decrease carbs elsewhere. Sugar makes blood glucose levels rise quickly because it goes straight to the bloodstream. Starches and other complex carbohydrates convert to sugar during digestion, so they take longer to reach the bloodstream. What is important is the total amount of carbohydrates eaten, not the type, so if a person wants to eat a piece of pie for dessert, he may have to skip the potato during his meal. However, people should not make a habit of substituting a

## What Is Hypoglycemia?

For those on insulin or some oral medications, exercising too hard, taking too much insulin, missing a meal, or not eating enough carbohydrates can make blood glucose levels take a nosedive—a condition called hypoglycemia. When this happens, people become shaky, irritable, sweaty, uncoordinated, and confused. Without treatment, they can experience seizures and loss of consciousness. At that point, hypoglycemia becomes a medical emergency.

The American Diabetes Association (ADA) considers glucose levels below 70 mg/dl to be hypoglycemia. This condition is not rare. The ADA estimates that people with type 1 diabetes have episodes once or twice a week (the condition is less common in people with type 2 diabetes). Most diabetics, though, know how to treat the condition before it becomes dangerous. They always carry a fast-acting sugar such as glucose tablets (available in drugstores), jelly beans, gumdrops, raisins, or sugar packets, and consume this source of glucose as soon as they notice symptoms. The symptoms usually subside, and the individual usually feels better, within minutes.

People with diabetes also need to alert their friends and coworkers about the symptoms of hypoglycemia so they can help out if necessary. Many people have been mistaken for drunks because the symptoms are so similar to those of alcoholic intoxication. People with diabetes should also wear a medical identification bracelet or necklace that identifies them as having diabetes and lists their name and an emergency phone number.

sugary food with little nutritional value for a carbohydrate that contains lots of vitamins, minerals, and fiber.

## FIBER, FATS, AND PROTEIN

Everyone should eat 20 to 35 grams of fiber a day. Examples of high-fiber foods are apples with skins, bran, beans, and oatmeal. Two types of fiber exist: soluble and insoluble. Insoluble fiber is not broken down during digestion and is thought to lower blood glucose levels, though experts are not sure exactly how. Soluble fiber is broken down and absorbed by the body.

Fats are also important, but only polyunsaturated fats like olive oil and canola oil are "heart-healthy"; that is, they do not contribute to cardiovascular disease. Omega-3 fats, which help protect the heart, are particularly good for you. Trout, salmon, mackerel, and herring are the best sources of omega-3. Foods high in saturated fats and cholesterol should be eaten in moderation because they clog arteries and contribute to heart disease. Some of these foods are red meat, whole-milk dairy products, coconut and palm oils, and egg yolks. Trans fats are man-made fats and are solid at room temperature. Found in margarines and partially hydrogenated oils, trans fats raise cholesterol and should be avoided.

Protein should account for 15 to 20 percent of a person's diet, according to the ADA. People with diabetes need the same amount of protein as people without diabetes, unless they have kidney damage. People with kidney problems are advised to eat less protein to help slow the damage.

## TRANSPLANT SURGERY

Researchers continue to look for easier and better ways to treat diabetes. Transplant surgery is the most dramatic treatment method available today, and perhaps the most promising.

In type 1 diabetes, the immune system destroys the beta cells that make insulin in the pancreas. Getting the beta cells working again sounds like the perfect solution, but so far, this has stumped researchers. However, they have come up with an alternative: pancreas transplantation, or replacing the malfunctioning pancreas with a new one. Since 1988, more than 5,600 pancreas transplants have been performed in the United States.[9]

Unfortunately, the process is complicated. The surgery is risky, expensive, and best performed on patients under age 45 who are in relatively good health. A donor must also be available. Because people have only one pancreas, the organ comes from a deceased person, and the wait can be long. However, a close living relative may donate part of his pancreas, usually along with one of his kidneys, since people with type 1 diabetes often have severe kidney disease, too. This is called a pancreas-kidney transplant. More than

Liver

Pancreatic islet

Pancreas

Beta cell

Pancreatic transplant surgery, in which beta cells from pancreatic islets are replaced, is a promising new technique.

14,800 of these procedures have been performed in the United States since 1988.[10]

But even if the transplant surgery goes well, there are still pitfalls. When a person receives someone else's organ, the immune system treats the new organ as a foreign invader and attacks it. Consequently, people with transplants must take powerful drugs called immunosuppressants for the rest of their lives to keep their bodies from rejecting the new organ. Still, up to half of all pancreas transplants are rejected.[11] Immunosuppressants also make people more susceptible to other diseases, such as cancer and viral infections. So even though a successful pancreas transplant means the end of insulin injections, people still have to take strong drugs for the rest of their lives. Researchers continue to look for the perfect solution.

# CHAPTER SIX

# Outlook for the Future

nsulin was developed in 1922, and it revolutionized diabetes treatment. Without it, an estimated 15 million people living with the disease today would have died at an early age.[1] Even so, since the 1930s, researchers have been looking hard for ways to prevent or cure diabetes, as well as for better and easier ways to diagnose and treat it.

Right now, thousands of diabetes studies are being conducted around the world. Drugs and vaccines are being tested, surgical procedures are being perfected, and better equipment is being developed to make managing diabetes easier. So far, nothing has equaled the discovery of insulin, but researchers are solving the mysteries of diabetes and moving slowly but surely toward a breakthrough.

Researchers are still seeking new ways to prevent and cure diabetes.

## ADVANCES IN MANAGEMENT

People with diabetes stay healthy by keeping their blood glucose levels under control. Needles, pumps, and meters help them manage their diabetes, but equipment design and accuracy can always be improved.

### New Insulin Delivery Systems

Until a scientific breakthrough occurs, insulin remains the first-line treatment for type 1 diabetes. Researchers continue to search for ways to eliminate needles and make the administration of insulin painless and more convenient. Alternatives currently being explored include insulin pills, patches, and inhalers. Pills and patches are still in the experimental stage, but an insulin inhaler called Exubera® did reach the consumer market in 2006. Although the inhaler was the first alternative to needles since insulin was discovered, it was not widely adopted.

Exubera's manufacturer thought the inhaler filled with powdered insulin would be a popular and successful product. But sales were so disappointing that the company discontinued the drug in late 2007. A number of factors made it unpopular. Users found the inhaler was awkward to handle. Many doctors were not convinced the device could deliver insulin in precise doses like a needle or insulin pump, and so they did not often prescribe it. Exubera only delivered rapid-acting insulin for use before meals, so patients still had to inject long-acting insulin at other times during the day.[2]

The Seven System, produced by DexCom, Inc., continuously monitors glucose. It consists of a tiny disposable sensor inserted under the skin of the abdomen, a small wireless transmitter attached to an adhesive "pod" that sits on top of the skin over the sensor, and a receiver that can be worn on a belt. The sensor can be used for up to seven days before a new one must be inserted with a special needle.[3]

Today, two other needleless delivery systems are currently being tested: one that sprays liquid insulin into the mouth and one that sprays it into the nostrils. Both of these devices are several years away from being approved by the Food and Drug Administration (FDA), which tests and permits the sale of drugs in the United States.

Insulin patches are still being tested and FDA approval is pending. They consist of an insulin-impregnated patch that attaches to the skin with adhesive, a transmitter that fits on top of the patch, and a rechargeable battery system. Sound waves from the transmitter push the insulin through the skin into the bloodstream. Like an insulin pump, the patch can be programmed to deliver a continuous low dose of insulin throughout the day.

# Sound waves from the insulin patch's transmitter push the insulin through the skin into the bloodstream.

Insulin pills could be an excellent delivery system, but problems have arisen in making them effective. When a person swallows insulin, it is destroyed by the digestive system before it can even reach the bloodstream. Researchers are experimenting with a gel-like coating to cover the pill and protect the insulin from stomach acid. However, some experts question the usefulness of insulin in pill form because many people take several different doses of insulin in one day and would require pills of varying strengths, which could prove confusing and inconvenient.

## Improved Insulin Pumps

The first insulin pump, developed in 1963 by Dr. Arnold Kadish, was worn in a backpack and looked like a prop from a science fiction movie. It proved to be too impractical to wear. Over the years, external insulin pumps, which are worn outside the body, were continually redesigned, becoming smaller and easier to use, until they are now the size of a cell phone.

One new external pump, the OmniPod, adheres to the stomach and delivers insulin to the body through a small attached tube. The "pod" is refilled with insulin every three days. It comes with a wireless blood glucose meter that fits in the hand.

Implantable pumps are the new kids on the block. Inserted under the skin of the stomach, they deliver insulin in short, frequent pulses. There are no external tubes, and insulin doses are programmed with a handheld remote control. These pumps are still being tested in the United States, but one, the Medtronic Model 2007, is already on the market in Europe. Implantable pumps are thought to work especially well for type 1 diabetes patients who have trouble controlling their glucose levels.[4]

Implantable pumps take researchers several steps closer to their goal of developing an artificial pancreas— a surgically implanted pump that would sense a rise in blood glucose levels and automatically release the correct amount of insulin—just like a real pancreas.

## Better Glucose Monitoring Systems

Studies show that people with type 1 and type 2 diabetes feel better and reduce their risk of long-term complications by checking their blood glucose levels frequently. In fact, the term "aggressive" is often used to describe the best approach to self-monitoring. More than a dozen new glucose meters are now available. There are models that check both blood glucose levels and blood pressure, "talking" meters that give test results verbally in both English and Spanish, meters with alarms that warn of low blood glucose levels, and meters that store up to 450 tests so people can compare their readings over time.

The latest innovation is the continuous glucose monitor. A sensor inserted under the skin of the stomach measures the level of glucose in the tissue every 10 seconds, then wirelessly sends the readings to a device the size of a pager

that can be worn on a belt. The monitor averages readings every 5 minutes, 24 hours a day, and sounds an alarm if glucose readings get too high or too low. Two companies are making the

Many blood glucose monitors are now available, including models that "talk" and/or store past tests for comparison.

sensor, which was approved by the FDA in 2007. The device is designed to point out trends in glucose levels, such as dangerous overnight lows or early morning spikes. It is not meant to replace regular glucose monitoring.

## New Drugs for Type 2 Diabetes

New, more effective drugs are being developed to help people with type 2 diabetes control their blood glucose levels without injecting insulin. Studies are trying to determine if combining these pills with diet and exercise is the best way to manage type 2 diabetes and prevent people from eventually having to take insulin. Some pills available now increase the amount of insulin made by the pancreas or decrease the amount of glucose released by the liver. A new type of drug called a

DPP-4 inhibitor does both of these things. Drugs called sulfonylureas can be even more effective.

Unfortunately, some new drugs may have serious side effects. In May 2007, the FDA issued a safety alert on rosiglitazone maleate, sold under the names Avandia® and Actos®, because some patients taking it developed heart failure. The drug's manufacturers have since placed a warning about these problems on the drug's label.[5]

## INCHING TOWARD A CURE

When Banting and Best discovered insulin in 1922, they probably never dreamed we would still be searching for a cure in the twenty-first century. One stumbling block is that diabetes is an autoimmune disease, and scientists still do not fully understand why the immune system attacks its own organs and tissues. When they finally unlock the secrets of autoimmune disorders, they could prevent or reverse diabetes and possibly do the same with dozens of other autoimmune diseases.

Diabetes is an autoimmune disease, and scientists still do not fully understand why the immune system attacks its own organs and tissues.

In addition, if autoimmunity were better understood, organ transplant recipients would not have to take powerful drugs for the rest of their lives to prevent their bodies from rejecting the new organs. This would greatly benefit people with diabetes who undergo pancreas transplants, pancreas-kidney transplants, or islet cell transplants, and is an important research goal.

## SAY what

## What Are Stem Cells?

Stem cells can develop into any other type of cell in the body. They are found in umbilical cord blood and in human embryos that have just been fertilized. Smaller amounts of these cells are also found in adult bone marrow, brain, skin, liver, and other tissues. Researchers are experimenting with how to induce these cells to develop in certain ways. Embryonic stem cells are thought to work the best for this type of effort, but some people are opposed to their use on ethical grounds.

Stem cell research on animals is being done in laboratories around the world, but it will be many years before these techniques can be tested on humans.

Still, the amazing ability of stem cells to morph into muscle, nerve, brain, blood, or islet cells could help cure many diseases, including type 1 diabetes. If scientists could make stem cells grow into islet cells, they could be transplanted into people whose pancreases have stopped producing insulin. Patients would no longer need a complete pancreas transplant, nor would two donor pancreases be needed for an islet cell transplant.

Stem cells can develop into any type of cell—including islet cells.

Other cure-related research is focused on islet cell transplantation, the use of stem cells, and the development of an artificial pancreas.

## Islet Cell Transplantation

In the pancreas, the islets of Langerhans contain cells that produce insulin and deal out just the right amount into the blood. These cells are also the ones that get destroyed in type 1 diabetes. However, they make up only a small proportion of the entire pancreas. It appears that transplanting only the islet cells could make more sense than transplanting the whole pancreas.

Two doctors from the University of Alberta in Edmonton, Canada, thought this made sense, too. In 2000, they introduced the islet cell transplantation procedure in use today, called the Edmonton Protocol.

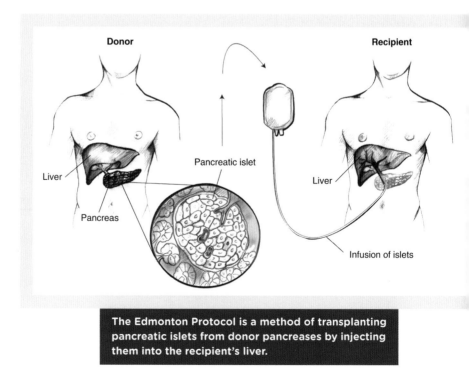

The Edmonton Protocol is a method of transplanting pancreatic islets from donor pancreases by injecting them into the recipient's liver.

In this protocol, pancreases are obtained from two deceased donors. The pancreases are treated with a special enzyme that helps separate thousands of fragile islet cells so they can be removed. After removal, the surgeon inserts a tube into the patient's lower stomach and then slowly injects the islets through the tube into the liver. Two or three separate injections of islets are necessary.

Afterward, three anti-rejection drugs are given to suppress the immune system. One drug is given immediately; the other two must be taken by the patient for life, or for as long as the islets continue to work. Because these drugs can have serous side effects, including kidney problems and an increased chance of cancer, researchers are trying to find ways to transplant islet cells successfully without these drugs. For example, some researchers are experimenting with a special coating on islet cells to see if this helps prevent them from being rejected.

Islet cells can be transplanted by injecting them into the body through a tube. This procedure is still experimental but holds great promise.

Since 2000, several hundred islet cell transplants have been done using the Edmonton Protocol. However, the procedure is still considered experimental and is only used for people with severe diabetes that cannot be kept under control. It is also only temporarily effective. A year after surgery, most people can abandon insulin.

After five years, they usually have to return to insulin, either because the new islets have quit working or the immunosuppressant drugs have damaged them. Researchers are working on ways to prevent these problems.

In 2006, the Collaborative Islet Transplant Registry reported the results of 23 islet transplant programs involving 225 people from 1999 to 2005. Six months after a transplant, more than half were still off insulin, but after two years, only one-third were insulin-free. On the plus side, those back on insulin did not need as much, had better blood glucose control, and had fewer episodes of severe hypoglycemia than before their transplants.[6]

The best way to prevent type 2 diabetes is a combination of exercise and a low-calorie, low-fat diet.

### Artificial Pancreas

An artificial pancreas consists of a sensor and an insulin pump that are implanted under the skin by a surgeon. Called a closed-loop system, the device imitates a real pancreas by constantly checking glucose levels in the blood, calculating the amount of insulin needed, and then automatically releasing just the right dose. It would reduce the burden of managing diabetes by letting a machine do most of the work and also help people with type 1 diabetes keep tighter glucose control.

The Juvenile Diabetes Research Foundation supports the development of an artificial pancreas, which many believe would revolutionize diabetes management. The foundation is funding millions of dollars worth of research. Several manufacturers are working on trial products of the artificial pancreas, and clinical trials are being held to test the system in children and adults.

Because the system is totally internal and automatic, there is very little tolerance for error. Machinery or programming could malfunction and miscalculate a dosage or break down completely. In the meantime, the person's blood glucose levels could fluctuate dangerously. These concerns affect the FDA's eventual approval of such a device.[7]

## ADVANCES IN PREVENTION

Most of the cutting-edge equipment and advanced surgical procedures discussed in this chapter are designed to help people with type 1 diabetes. But people with type 2 diabetes are not being neglected. More is being learned about the role of diet and exercise and about the relationship between genes, obesity, and type 2 diabetes.

As for preventing type 1 diabetes, research is being conducted on insulin pills and telltale genes and antibodies. Scientists are trying to find ways to stop both types of diabetes before they start.

## Ali and Marissa: Twins on a Mission

When 13-year-old Ali Newman got home from summer camp, her parents and twin sister, Marissa, were shocked. Instead of looking healthy, Ali looked tired and skinny. She had lost ten pounds and was so exhausted she kept falling asleep in the car and even at her friends' homes.

Ali's family and friends kept asking her what was wrong, but she could not tell them because she had no idea herself. She felt especially frustrated when people accused her of having an eating disorder because she knew that was not her problem.

Ali was feeling worse than ever in September, when the family went to visit relatives and celebrate the Jewish New Year. One night, she could barely walk up the stairs she was so exhausted. "I'd go two steps, then stop and take a breath," Ali remembered.[8]

Worried, Marissa stayed up all night, watching over Ali while she slept. When Ali woke up and said she was too weak to even walk down the hall, Marissa called her parents and asked them to take her twin sister to the hospital.

When they arrived in the emergency room at 3 A.M., Ali was barely conscious. A blood test revealed that her blood glucose level was sky high. She had a life-threatening condition called diabetic ketoacidosis caused by type 1 diabetes. Her parents and sister were shocked.

In the emergency room, Ali was given insulin and recovered. Two years later, she is managing her diabetes well, feeling healthy, and cheering on the varsity cheerleading squad. But the story does not end here.

After Ali's diagnosis, Marissa learned that she was also at risk for type 1 diabetes. Because she and Ali are fraternal twins (they do not share exactly the same genes), the risk is not as great as with identical twins, whose genetic makeup is exactly the same. Still, getting type 1 diabetes was a very real possibility. So Ali's doctor approached Marissa with an idea: Would she be willing to join a national TrialNet study to see if type 1 diabetes could be prevented or delayed with pills? Marissa and her parents eagerly agreed, and she became the first person to enroll in the study in February 2007.

In the TrialNet study, half of the subjects take a daily insulin pill and the other half take a placebo. Subjects are not told which group they are in. For four years, they will take the pills and get checked regularly. In the end, the results will be compared to see how many in each group developed type 1 diabetes.

Marissa did not think twice about enrolling. "If a person has the opportunity and fits the criteria, I think it's the most helpful thing you can do right now," she said. "I thought, 'Why wouldn't I do this?' It opens a lot of doors for other things."[9]

Before the TrialNet study, people at risk for diabetes had to just wait and hope for the best. With the TrialNet study, that may be changing.

## TYPE 2 DIABETES

The good news about type 2 diabetes is that it can usually be prevented by healthy eating and exercise. The bad news is that too many people are either not aware of this fact or are ignoring it. The federal government believes educating the public is the best way to prevent type 2 diabetes and has launched the National Diabetes Education Program. People can log onto their Web site for free information and downloads.

Research is being conducted on the role of drugs and genes in preventing type 2 diabetes.

**Drugs:** So far, no drug has been approved by the FDA to prevent type 2 diabetes. However, studies have been done to see if the drugs used to *treat* type 2 diabetes can help lower blood glucose levels in people with prediabetes. The conclusion? A low-calorie, low-fat diet combined with exercise is still the safest and most effective way to prevent the disease.

**Genes:** In 2007, British researchers studied 2,000 people with type 2 diabetes, looking for a link between genes and the disease. They discovered changes (mutations) in one gene, called the FTO gene, in overweight people with diabetes. This change is called a gene variant. To double check, they studied an additional 38,759 children and adults from England, Finland, and Italy and found a similar link between weight and the FTO gene variant. This was the first time a specific gene had been linked both to obesity and type 2 diabetes. However, the research team stressed that genes alone do not cause obesity or type 2 diabetes; lifestyle and environment also play a part.[10]

A total of ten genes have been connected with type 2 diabetes. The most recent discovery is a TCF7L2 gene variant. In a study of people in Iceland, Denmark, and the United States, one-third were found to have one copy of the gene and 7 percent had two copies. Researchers calculate that this gene causes about 20 percent of all cases of type 2 diabetes and that people with two copies have a 141 percent greater risk of developing type 2 diabetes.[11]

## TYPE 1 DIABETES

Studies are being done to investigate the role of drugs, antibodies, and genes in preventing type 1 diabetes.

**Drugs:** Can an insulin pill prevent or delay type 1 diabetes? One study conducted by the NIH in the

TrialNet program aims to find out. This clinical trial is being conducted in more than 100 medical centers in the United States, Canada, Europe, and Australia. All the subjects have antibodies to insulin in their blood already. Half the subjects take an insulin pill every day and the other half take a placebo. Although oral insulin can't regulate blood sugar levels because it is broken down too quickly, experts think that perhaps when the pill goes through the digestive tract it will reduce the antibody response to insulin through repeated exposure. This may calm the immune system so it does not attack and destroy the islet cells in the pancreas. This destruction can start up to ten years before type 1 diabetes is even diagnosed.

Subjects are people from one to forty-five years old who have close relatives with type 1 diabetes and are therefore at high risk for the disease. A simple blood test shows if they have various types of antibodies in their blood that might destroy islet cells.

A second study within TrialNet is for people twelve to thirty-five years old who have been diagnosed with type 1 diabetes within the last three months. Newly diagnosed people usually still have some functioning islet cells, and the study is testing a drug that might preserve these cells.[12]

**Antibodies:** Until recently, three different types of antibodies had been identified that destroy islet cells. In October 2007, researchers in Denver, Colorado, announced they had discovered a fourth antibody, called ZnTB. When three antibodies are found in a person's

Scientists continue to explore the link between genes, ethnicity, and diabetes.

blood, the chance of getting diabetes is 90 percent. The fourth antibody increases the prediction rate to 96 percent. This was the first new diabetes-predicting antibody to be discovered in ten years. Experts hope the discovery of new antibodies in the blood will lead to a better understanding of how the immune system works and allow detection of diabetes in very young children before fluctuating blood glucose causes any damage.[13]

**Genes:** Genes also play a role in type 1 diabetes, but not as great as in type 2. Scientists have found changes in genes that greatly increase the risk of developing type 1 diabetes. In most cases, people have to inherit a susceptibility to the disease from both parents, and some experts think white people are more susceptible than other races because more of them have the disease. Most white people with type 1 diabetes have variations on the HLA-DR3 or HLA-DR4 genes, which affect the immune response.[14]

## IMPACT OF DIABETES ON SOCIETY

Great strides have been made in the diagnosis, management, and treatment of diabetes, and research on genes and autoimmunity is making a cure a real possibility. But around the world, the number of people with diabetes continues to grow, and treatment can be expensive. According to the International Diabetes Federation there are tremendous disparities in the availability of treatment, mainly due to cost.

- In 2007, diabetes was estimated to have caused 3.8 million deaths, about equal to HIV/AIDS.
- People in the poorest countries have the highest death rates, and children die because they cannot afford insulin. For example, the life expectancy of an insulin-dependent diabetic in Mozambique, Africa, is only twelve months.
- Only 8 percent of all the people with diabetes in the world live in the United States, but fifty percent of the money spent on diabetes worldwide is spent here.
- Twenty-five percent of the money spent worldwide on diabetes is spent in Europe; most of the rest is spent in Australia, Japan, and other industrialized countries.
- The poorest countries in the world do not have enough money to provide even the cheapest diabetes medicines.
- At least $232 billion was spent worldwide in 2007 to treat and prevent diabetes and its complications.[15]

In 2007, diabetes was estimated to have caused 3.8 million deaths, about equal to HIV/AIDS.

The American Diabetes Association offers these statistics about the United States:

- Diabetes is the sixth leading cause of death.
- The yearly cost of diabetes was $132 billion in 2002, twice what it was in 1992.
- The medical care for each person with diabetes costs $13,243, compared to $2,560 for people who do not have diabetes. This includes money spent by people, employers, insurance companies, and Medicare and Medicaid.
- The most expensive complication of diabetes is cardiovascular disease, which includes heart attacks and strokes.[16]

The economic toll of diabetes can be expressed in billions of dollars, but the personal toll is incalculable. Even in developed countries like the United States, people with diabetes and their families can have overwhelming expenses for drugs, equipment, and hospitalizations and feel the burden of reduced income and productivity from lost work time, disability from complications, and early death.

According to the International Diabetes Federation, rates of diabetes are increasing even faster in poor countries, which often have inadequate health care. Drugs such as insulin are often too expensive to buy or difficult to obtain.

In the United States, the Centers for Disease Control and Prevention (CDC), a government agency, has launched education programs to teach people about ways to prevent and treat diabetes and to make sure people get good health care. In 2006, the federal government allotted about $63 million for the diabetes program. It also funds research, including studies verifying that exercise and a healthy diet can reduce the risk of type 2 diabetes. Other programs target young people, American Indians and Alaska Natives, and other groups of high-risk people to try to prevent or treat the disease and slow down the epidemic.[17]

# CHAPTER SEVEN

# Living with Diabetes

**D**iabetes has been referred to as "the thinking person's disease"; not because thinking causes it, but because people with diabetes must always think.[1] Every day, no matter where they are or how busy they are, people with diabetes test their blood glucose levels, inject themselves with insulin or program their insulin pumps, and calculate how much insulin they need to offset the carbohydrates they will eat. They do this at work, at school, at the gym, and when they are out with friends. Diabetics cannot take a day off from diabetes.

Having diabetes means always thinking and planning ahead.

## Diabetics cannot take a day off from diabetes.

People with type 2 diabetes may not require insulin and may need to check their blood glucose levels only twice a day, but they still must follow a healthy diet, exercise regularly, and often take oral diabetes medicine. Like people with type 1 diabetes, they need to plan ahead and do a lot more thinking about everyday things than nondiabetics.

Besides their everyday responsibilities, the lives of people with diabetes become a balancing act of food-insulin, exercise-insulin, and so on. Most manage well, but challenges occur daily, both for people with diabetes and their families.

## COMMON CHALLENGES

Diabetes impacts every part of a person's life, from their work life to their sex life. Here are some areas of concern.

### Working with Diabetes

Fitting diabetes care into a workday is not always easy. People with 9-to-5 jobs in offices may not have much trouble managing their diabetes. They can keep supplies and snacks in their desk, go to the restroom to test their blood glucose levels or inject insulin, and take their lunch breaks at a regular time. But people whose work schedules vary, who work the night shift, travel, or who do not have desk jobs can find managing diabetes more difficult.

For example, someone who works outdoors, like a landscaper, may have to inject insulin while in his car, and a nurse in a doctor's office may get so busy with patients she does not have time for lunch. Diabetics can adjust to almost any schedule with careful planning, but need frequent blood glucose monitoring to see how a plan is working.

People with diabetes can work at almost any job if they are qualified, with two exceptions: According to U.S. law, they cannot serve in the military or pilot a commercial airplane because of the possibility of dangerous blood sugar fluctuations. Thanks to efforts by the American Diabetes Association (ADA), they can now pilot small, private aircraft and also drive a bus or truck from state to state.[2]

## Going to School with Diabetes

Some parents worry about sending their children with diabetes to school. Will they be safe? Will they be treated differently from other students?

"Be prepared" is the best motto. Parents should talk to teachers and school administrators to learn about policies for handling the needs of children with diabetes. They should also develop a diabetes management plan with their child's doctor and present it to the school where it can be adapted so the student can manage his diabetes and the school staff can handle an emergency.

Unfortunately, not all schools are doing a good job helping students with diabetes. For example, some do not allow students to test their blood glucose levels in class or at school activities; others do not have staff members trained to handle an emergency, so they rely on calling 911. In 2005, the ADA initiated the Safe at School Campaign to try to remedy this situation.[3]

## Traveling with Diabetes

Before they travel, people with diabetes need to plan ahead a bit more than others. They should pack their diabetes supplies carefully in their carry-on bag in case their luggage is lost and bring extra supplies in case they are away longer than expected. If they use an insulin pump, they should bring syringes and needles in case their pump stops working. A letter from their doctor will help them get through security checkpoints more easily; so will clearly labeling their insulin, glucagon, and other supplies. If they are traveling to a non-English-speaking country, they should learn to say, "I have diabetes. Sugar or orange juice, please," in that country's language. And of course, they should always wear a medical identification necklace or bracelet.

## Dining with Diabetes

People with diabetes enjoy food, and they sometimes eat "special occasion" foods that are way at the top of the food pyramid. They rarely eat anything without doing some quick calculations in their head. For example, if they want a slice of pepperoni pizza after a movie, they will subtract some carbohydrates at dinner.

Jake Benner knows how to balance carbohydrates and insulin. "Two pieces of pizza are about 48 grams of carbs, and I'm supposed to take 1 unit of insulin for every 8 carbs," he said. He obviously likes pizza and eats it often, so he has memorized the figures.[4]

A vegetable salad is a healthy, low-carb choice.

People can also plan ahead by finding out what food Grandma is serving for Christmas dinner or by calling a restaurant to ask about daily specials or whether the chef can prepare a special meal. Books and Web sites provide the carbohydrate content of foods in grams, including foods from fast food restaurants. With a little advance planning, people hardly ever get caught unprepared.

Insulin pumps make it easier for people to indulge. They just program in the amount of carbohydrates they plan to eat and the pump automatically adjusts the dosage of insulin.

### Exercising with Diabetes

Exercise keeps people fit and trim and helps blood glucose levels stay in line by using up the stored glucose in the muscles, liver, and blood. But in some, exercise can cause problems if it makes glucose levels plummet. Once again, planning ahead is the solution. Intense aerobic exercise such as running causes faster drops in blood glucose than activities such as weight training. Regular exercisers with diabetes who take insulin are good at estimating how active they will be and adjusting their food and insulin. They monitor before, after, and sometimes even during exercise to avoid hypoglycemia.

Aerobic exercise is important, but people with diabetes must be careful to monitor their insulin levels when they exercise.

They also drink lots of water and carry a quick source of carbohydrates such as glucose tablets. Some people with type 2 diabetes are not at risk for low blood sugar, even during or after exercise, depending on which medications they take.

## Intense aerobic exercise such as running causes faster drops in blood glucose than activities such as weight training.

Tesch West, featured in Chapter 4, found that her blood glucose falls about four hours after exercising and then again up to twelve hours afterwards. She knows to eat more at those times. "It's a bummer, because exercise is so important," she said.[5]

## INSULIN SHOCK OR DIABETIC COMA?

Severely high or severely low blood glucose can cause coma, a life-threatening condition. Coma caused by low blood glucose levels is also called "severe hypoglycemia," by medical professionals and "insulin shock," or "insulin reaction" by lay people. It occurs because too much insulin in the bloodstream has removed too much blood glucose and can progress to seizures and death. Causes include not eating, taking too much insulin or too many pills for type 2 diabetes, stress, and heavy exercise. Coma caused by high blood glucose levels is called "severe hyperglycemia," or "diabetic coma" and occurs because of too little insulin in the bloodstream. It can also be fatal. Causes include not taking enough insulin or pills, eating too much sugar, stress, and infection.

Glucagon or sugar will help a person in insulin shock, but not diabetic coma. A person in diabetic coma needs insulin, but sugar will not harm him. In either case, call 911! Here is a comparison of the signs of insulin shock and diabetic coma:

| Insulin Shock (severe hypoglycemia) | Diabetic Coma (hyperglycemia) |
|---|---|
| Occurs rapidly | Occurs over hours or days |
| Pale skin | Nausea and vomiting |
| Cold sweats | Confusion |
| Rapid pulse | Deep, fast breathing |
| Rapid breathing | Thirst |
| Dizziness | Dehydration |

| Insulin Shock (severe hypoglycemia) | Diabetic Coma (hyperglycemia) |
| --- | --- |
| Weakness | Fever |
| Double vision or blurry vision | Headache |
| Headache | Abdominal pain |
| Numbness in hands and feet | Fatigue |
| Hunger | Muscle aches or stiffness |
| Confusion | Mental stupor |
| Irritability (even combativeness) | Breathing difficulty when lying down |
| Nervousness | Sweet or fruity-smelling breath |
| Trembling | Drowsiness |
| Hallucinations | |

Student athletes often discover that their coaches have a limited understanding of diabetes. For example, wrestling coaches might instruct students, including those with diabetes, to "make weight" (conform to weight class guidelines) by dieting (not a good idea). Some coaches might also recommend power bars, energy drinks, or protein supplements. These foods are often very high in carbohydrates, so diabetic students should check with their doctors before using them.

## Pregnancy and Diabetes

Women with type 1 or type 2 diabetes who plan to become pregnant should keep their blood glucose levels well-controlled even before pregnancy. High blood glucose during pregnancy increases the risk of birth defects. This is especially true during the first two months, when the baby's nervous system, arms and legs, and organs are developing. Pregnant women with diabetes are also more prone to miscarriage (pregnancy that ends before the fetus can survive outside the uterus).

Gestational diabetes occurs more than halfway through a pregnancy in women who did not have diabetes before. By this time, the baby is almost fully developed, but the extra glucose in the mother's blood can make the baby grow very large. Most women with gestational diabetes can keep their blood glucose levels in check with a meal plan and exercise.

### Getting Sick with Diabetes

A cold or a case of the flu can be a big deal for someone with diabetes. Illness stresses the body and makes it release hormones to fight infection. Unfortunately, these hormones can make blood glucose levels rise dangerously. People with diabetes need to monitor their blood glucose more often when they are sick and also check their urine for ketones, chemicals produced when the body burns fats for energy instead of glucose. The appearance of ketones means not enough insulin is available to break down glucose. Extra insulin must be taken immediately or the condition can progress to a coma and even death.

Taking cold medicines can also be tricky. Some over-the-counter decongestants contain ingredients that raise blood glucose levels; other medicines contain sugar and alcohol. People with diabetes need to check with the pharmacist or their doctor before taking these drugs.

People with diabetes can end up with serious complications from a cold or flu. To try to prevent this, the ADA recommends that all people with diabetes receive preventive immunizations: a yearly flu shot and a one-time-only pneumonia shot.[6]

## CHALLENGES FOR TEENAGERS

Teenagers with diabetes have many of the concerns discussed above, as well as a whole other set of concerns specific to their age group, from dating to dieting.

### The Dating Game

Teenagers usually hang out with a close circle of friends. Other than their families, these are the people who know them best. Most teens with diabetes feel comfortable enough with their disease, and their friends, to share this part of their life. On the practical side, they also want people they can depend on if they have low blood glucose and need help. A teen with a positive attitude about diabetes will help his friends take the news in stride.

Diabetes will not shake a strong relationship with a caring boyfriend or girlfriend.

Telling a boyfriend or girlfriend about diabetes is a little harder. What if they are turned off by the idea of needles, pumps, and meters? Since keeping all the paraphernalia hidden is next to impossible, most teens just get the announcement out of the way as soon as possible. Part of growing up is discovering who they are and what kind of people they want to be friendly with. Diabetes is not who a person is, and a good friend will know this.

# What if a boyfriend or girlfriend is turned off by the idea of needles, pumps, and meters?

### Driving Safely

Getting a driver's license is a rite of passage for teenagers, but those with diabetes must take special precautions. Rule number one is to test their blood glucose before driving. Some people have told interviewers that driving with low blood sugar feels like being drunk![7] On long trips, drivers should check glucose every two hours and pull over and have a snack if they feel "low." Keeping crackers and other snacks in the car as well as glucose tablets is a must. Traveling with a friend is a good idea, too. Also, glucose meters, test strips, and insulin are sensitive to temperature changes and should not be left in a hot or cold car.

### Drinking, Smoking, and Illegal Drugs

Everyone knows that drinking and driving are a deadly combination. But people with diabetes do not have to get behind the wheel to have serious consequences from alcohol. Alcohol has no nutritional value and can make

## Jake: Aware and In Control

When six-year-old Jake Benner* said he wanted to "burn down the school," his parents knew something was terribly wrong. Jake had always loved school, but now he was acting frustrated and irritable. He was also urinating a lot. A friend tipped Jake's mom off: "I'll bet he has diabetes," she said. She knew the signs because her son had it.

She was right. Jake's doctor diagnosed him with type 1 diabetes and admitted him to the hospital. After he got home, Jake learned to give himself his own shots right away, with his mom supervising. "It made me feel better," he remembered.[8] He had a sweet tooth, so at first, it was hard not being able to eat ice cream whenever he wanted to. But as he got older, he read about diabetes and how the pancreas works, and it made him feel more in control. He also got an insulin pump, which allowed him more food choices and regulated his blood sugar levels better.

"He's very aware, probably because he was diagnosed so young," Mrs. Benner said. "He gets his cereal out of the box with a measuring cup every morning."[9]

This vigilance can be misunderstood by people who are not familiar with diabetes. Once, a friend of Jake's mom came for dinner. When Jake announced, "I'm taking a cup and a half of rice," the friend's jaw dropped. "She thought we were rationing food!" Mrs. Benner laughed.[10]

Like all people with diabetes, Jake has episodes of fluctuating blood sugar levels. At school, he tests his blood sugar in the nurse's office between classes or whenever he feels "low" or "high" and programs his pump to give him more or less insulin. He also

*Continued on next page*

Continued from previous page

carries glucose tablets for emergencies and wears a medical alert necklace. He knows his blood sugar can go up when he gets nervous before a test and go down when he competes in a wrestling match. But "for the most part, it just kind of happens for no reason," he admitted.[11]

His friends watch out for him. "They all worry about me a lot. When we go to the movies, they'll notice something's wrong before I do," Jake said.[12]

Besides wrestling, Jake snowboards and mountain bikes. When he was younger, he also played baseball and football. "Diabetes doesn't hold me back at all," he said.[13]

* Not his real name.

people with diabetes forget to take their insulin or get careless about what they eat. It also makes blood glucose levels drop because it interferes with the release of glucose from the liver. Diabetics can get sudden, severe hypoglycemia when they drink alcohol.

An occasional drink is fine for adults whose blood glucose levels are steady. But alcohol abuse can be deadly for anyone with diabetes. It can make the long-term complications, such as eye problems, heart disease, and nerve damage, even more severe and also damage the liver. Liver damage can cause blood glucose levels to become unpredictable.

Not drinking at all is the safest route for teenagers and young adults with diabetes. But once they are of legal age, if they do drink, they should eat something first. They should also choose light beer or light wine and check the carbohydrates on the label, limit themselves to two drinks, and check their blood glucose often. They should also wear a medical ID tag and make sure someone with them knows they have diabetes and how to treat low blood glucose.

Tobacco is bad for everyone, but even worse for people with diabetes. Diabetes can damage the heart and blood vessels, and so can nicotine, the addictive drug in tobacco. So smoking along with diabetes packs a double punch. People trying to kick the habit may get irritable, hungry, anxious, and have headaches. These are some of the same signs as hypoglycemia, so testing blood is critical.

Marijuana and other illegal drugs can cause increases in appetite and blood glucose, or decreases in blood glucose if a person gets high and forgets to eat. They can also lead to abuse, cause addiction, and have serious psychological, social, and legal consequences.

## CHALLENGES FOR FAMILIES

When someone has diabetes, their whole family starts living differently. People check labels when food shopping, eat meals at more regular times, and possibly even start exercising together. Maybe, just maybe, everyone gets healthier. This is the upside of living with diabetes.

The downside starts the minute a family member is diagnosed. People feel shocked, angry, sad, and even guilty. With all of their other responsibilities, people wonder where they will find the time and energy to care for and support a child or spouse with diabetes. Siblings worry that their lives will change when their brother or sister suddenly requires so much attention.

When researchers asked teenagers, "What advice would you give a kid just diagnosed with diabetes?" some of them said, "I'd tell them it gets easier."[9] That advice holds true for the whole family. Living with diabetes may be stressful at first, but it gets better with time. If all family members learn about the disease, share their feelings, and shoulder some household responsibilities, life becomes a lot easier for everyone. The ADA offers these suggestions for family members:

- Get an education in diabetes care.
- Be supportive, but don't take on the role of caretaker.
- Learn to listen without offering advice or criticism.
- Be flexible and open to new ways of eating and spending free time.
- Plan for emergencies.[14]

## Diabetes for a Day

Some people with diabetes have challenged a boyfriend, girlfriend, or best friend to have "diabetes for a day" (or longer). Although they cannot actually inject insulin or use an insulin pump, they can do everything else: test their glucose several times a day, count carbohydrates, plan meals, and eat at set times. Afterwards, they will understand better what a person with diabetes goes through on a daily basis.

## NEW WAYS OF EATING

Food issues can be the hardest to resolve and can cause tension in families who like the old ways of doing things. Today's families are on the run and do not always sit down and eat together. But regular mealtimes are critical for people with diabetes who must eat within a few minutes of injecting insulin. Besides getting used to new mealtime rituals, family members may find fewer sweets and snack foods in the cupboards and more vegetables in the refrigerator. They know this kind of eating is better for them, but old habits die hard.

Compromises can be reached by talking things over. For example, if the person with diabetes feels tempted by chips or cookies, he can ask the snackers in the house not to eat these foods around him.

"We all changed," said Anne Hadley, Brian's mother (see "How Real Teens Deal," page 98). "We eat better and look at labels to check carbs. Before, we just grabbed anything."[15]

Lori Benner agrees (see "How Real Teens Deal," pages 135–136). "You learn how to eyeball foods, what a cup looks like, how many carbs are in a slice of bread," she said. "I keep a food chart on the refrigerator

It may be hard for the whole family to cut down on high-carb foods, but everyone can benefit from the healthy eating that diabetes requires.

## Diabulemia

A frightening new eating disorder has emerged in teenage girls with type 1 diabetes. "Diabulemia" involves skipping insulin doses or taking less insulin to lose weight. This causes blood glucose levels to rise, leading to frequent urination and rapid weight loss. Short-term effects are tiredness, dehydration, and loss of muscle tissue; long-term effects are a higher risk for developing diabetic complications, such as blindness and heart disease.

Up to 30 percent of teenage girls with diabetes have skipped or limited insulin to lose weight, one study found. Other studies suggest that teenage girls with diabetes are more than twice as likely to have eating disorders including anorexia (severely restricting food) and bulimia (vomiting or using laxatives to lose weight). Why? Some researchers think the constant carbohydrate counting and strict care plans necessary with diabetes can lead people to become obsessed with food.[16]

and refer to it a lot. We're more aware of nutrition in general. You really become educated."[17]

### NEW WAYS OF COMMUNICATING

Once people get used to sitting down for meals together, they might have more time to express their feelings about how life has changed since one family member got diabetes. A mother with diabetes might explain that if she gets cranky, it may be from the diabetes or it may be from being tired. She can ask people to volunteer for various chores around the house. Siblings may complain that a child with diabetes gets all the attention. Talking things over can help.

## Depression and Diabetes

Everyone feels bummed out once in a while. But when people feel down in the dumps for more than a couple of weeks, cannot sleep or sleep all time, cannot concentrate, and feel hopeless or worthless, that condition is called clinical depression. It occurs more often and lasts longer in people with diabetes than in the general population and is often accompanied by anger, anxiety, and denial. These are all common feelings in people with diabetes, especially when they are first diagnosed. However, depression can occur any time, including several years after diagnosis.

Depressed people do not take care of themselves as well as those without depression. On the other hand, people with diabetes who *do* take care of themselves and feel healthy are depressed a lot less.

**People with diabetes can get depressed like anyone else, but they are much less likely to be depressed if they take good care of themselves.**

## TEENAGE TROUBLES

Teenagers can be the hardest to deal with, even if they have had diabetes for several years. They may already have problems with self-image; diabetes may only make things worse. They may feel flawed and worry about being accepted. They want to be independent, but that means managing their own diabetes. Talk about pressure!

Teenagers often act moody, difficult, and rebellious. Is it any wonder some of them rebel against diabetes, too? They may get haphazard about checking their blood glucose, fib about test results, "forget" to take insulin, or go on food binges.

A good approach is realizing that keeping their blood glucose levels on track is the ideal way to fit in and get on with their lives. It works a lot better than not taking care of themselves and ending up with severe hypoglycemia or diabetic ketoacidosis.

*   *   *

Most people with diabetes are coping well and living happy, healthy lives. But living well with diabetes takes time, effort, and determination. Until a cure is found, the challenge for people with diabetes is making sure this "thinking person's disease" interrupts their busy lives as little as possible.

# Diabetes Timeline

**1552 B.C.:** Ebers Papyrus, an Egyptian document, contains the first written description of diabetes.

**400 B.C.:** Susrata, an Indian physician, describes a malady that causes excessive urination, which he blames on gluttony.

**About 100 A.D.:** Name "diabetes" is coined by the Greek physician Aretaeus.

**1674:** English physician Thomas Willis tastes diabetics' urine and finds it is sweet. He adds "mellitus," meaning "honey sweet," to the word "diabetes," to create "diabetes mellitus."

**1709:** Swiss physician Johann Brunner removes dogs' pancreases and discovers the dogs have intense thirst and excessive urination.

**1776:** English physician Mathew Dobson shows that sugar is present in the urine and blood of people with diabetes, proving that the disorder involves the whole body, not just the kidneys.

**1788:** British researcher Thomas Crawley discovers a definite link between the pancreas and diabetes.

**1791:** German physician Johann Peter Frank develops a yeast test to detect sugar in urine, making taste testing a thing of the past.

**1797:** Scottish physician John Rollo introduces a high protein diet to treat diabetes.

**1857:** French physician Claude Bernard discovers that blood sugar levels are affected by a starch-like substance released by the liver, which he names "glucogen." This is the first time the liver was associated with diabetes.

**1869:** German medical student Paul Langerhans discovers "heaps of cells" in the pancreas. They are named the "islets of Langerhans" after his death in 1888.

**1889:** German physicians Oscar Minkowski and Joseph von Mering induce diabetes in dogs.

**1900:** American researcher Eugene Lindsay Opie discovers that deterioration of the islets of Langerhans leads to diabetes.

**1916:** English physician Sir Edward Sharpey-Schafer theorizes that the islets of Langerhans produce a substance that controls how the body uses carbohydrates. He calls this substance "insuline."

**1921:** Frederick Banting and Charles Best of Canada discover insulin.

**1922:** Leonard Thompson, age 14, becomes the first person to receive a successful insulin injection. Insulin starts being mass produced.

**1923:** The Nobel Prize for medicine and physiology is jointly awarded to Banting and J. J. R. Macleod.

**1930s:** Several new types of beef and pork insulins are developed.

**1935:** Roger Hinsworth discovers two types of diabetes: "insulin sensitive" (called type 1 today) and "insulin insensitive" (called type 2 today).

**1950s:** The first pill is developed to treat type 2 diabetes.

**1960s:** Urine strips are invented to test blood glucose levels.

**1966:** The first successful human pancreas transplant is performed at the University of Minnesota.

**Late 1970s:** The insulin pump is invented.

**1974:** The first islet cell transplant is performed, but the patient dies shortly afterwards

**1978:** The first synthetic (manmade) insulin is developed.

**1983:** Genetically engineered human insulin is put on the market.

**1986:** Blood glucose meters are approved for home use and eventually replace urine testing for most patients.

**1996:** Human insulin analogs are created.

**2000:** Canadian doctors introduce the Edmonton Protocol, now the standard procedure for islet cell transplants.

**2007:** Continuous glucose monitors are approved by the FDA.

# Chapter Notes

## Introduction

1. Centers for Disease Control and Prevention, "10 Leading Causes of Death All Populations, U.S, 2004," <http://www.cdc.gov/omhd/populations/multiracial.htm> (January 29, 2008).

2. International Diabetes Federation, "Did You Know?" <http://www.idf.org/home/index.cfm?unode=3B96906B-C026-2FD3-87B73F80BC22682A> (October 17, 2007).

3. Ibid.

4. American Diabetes Association, "Total Prevalence of Diabetes & Pre-diabetes," <http://diabetes.org/diabetes-statistics/prevalence.jsp> (January 30, 2008).

## Chapter 1: The Diabetes Dilemma

1. Interview with Kris Freeman, (December 20, 2007).

2. Ibid.

3. Ibid.

4. Ibid.

5. Ibid.

6. Ibid.

7. Ibid.

8. Ibid.

9. American Diabetes Association, "Total Prevalence of Diabetes & Pre-diabetes," <http://diabetes.org/diabetes-statistics/prevalence.jsp> (January 30, 2008).

10. International Diabetes Federation, "Did You Know?" <http://www.idf.org/home/index.cfm?unode=3B96906B-C026-2FD3-87B73F80BC22682A> (October 17, 2007).

11. Centers for Disease Control and Prevention, "Obesity and Overweight: Introduction," <http://www.cdc.gov/nccdphp/dnpa/obesity> (December 30, 2007).

12. Freeman.

13. Diabeteshealth.com, "Famous People with Diabetes," June 1, 2000, <http://www.diabeteshealth.com/read/2000/06/01/1929.html> (October 20, 2007).

14. Ibid.

## Chapter 2: The Science of Diabetes

1. *Agriculture Fact Book 2001–2002*, Chapter 2, "Profiling Food Consumption in America," United States Department of Agriculture, <http://www.usda.gov/factbook/index.html> (December 4, 2007).

2. Ibid.

3. Centers for Disease Control and Prevention, "National Diabetes Fact Sheet," January 31, 2005, <http://www.cdc.gov/diabetes/pubs/general.htm> (October 17, 2007).

4. *American Diabetes Association Complete Guide to Diabetes,* 4th edition, (New York: Bantam, 2006), p. 7.

5. R.J.Q. McNally, et al., "Space-time clustering analysis of type 1 diabetes among 0-29-year-olds in Yorkshire, UK," *Diabetologia,* May, 2006, pp. 9000–9004, <http://www.springerlink.com/content/2222743837050103/?p=0ef5f97d62fb4fe588e6ebd09b1b4d91&pi=10> (January 29, 2008).

6. *American Diabetes Association Complete Guide to Diabetes,* p. 7.

7. American Diabetes Association, "How to Tell If You Have Pre-Diabetes," <http://diabetes.org/pre-diabetes/pre-diabetes-symptoms.jsp> (January 3, 2008).

8. Ibid., p. 311.

9. Ibid., p. 318.

10. Ibid., p. 321.

11. Ibid., p. 325.

12. Childrenwithdiabetes.com, "Double Diabetes Summary," <http//:www.childrenwithdiabetes.com/type2/t2_dd.htm> (December 17, 2007).

13. National Diabetes Education Program, "Overview of Diabetes in Children and Adolescents," August, 2006, <http://ndep.nih.gov/diabetes/pubs/Youth_FactSheet.pdf> (January 22, 2008).

14. Diabetes.org, "How to Tell if You Have Pre-Diabetes," <www.diabetes.org/pre-diabetes/pre-diabetes-symptoms.jsp> (January 22, 2008).

15. Linda von Wartburg, "The Washington Boys and Their Activist Family Create a Diabetes Comic Book Superhero," *DiabetesHealth,* June 21, 2007, <www.diabeteshealth.com/read/2007/06/27/5288.html> (January 16, 2008).

16. Andale Gross, "Diabetic Teen and Brother Create Comics," *The Washington Post* and The Associated Press, May 27, 2007 <www.washingtonpost.com/wp-dyn/content/article/2007/05/26/AR2007052601421.html> (January 25, 2008).

## Chapter 3: The History of Diabetes

1. C. Savona-Ventura, "The History of Diabetes Mellitus: A Maltese Perspective," Diabetic Pregnancy Joint Clinic, Karin Grech Hospital, Malta, 2002, p. 4. <http://www.sahha.gov.mt/showdoc.aspx?id=589&filesource=4&file=history.pdf> (December, 20, 2007).

2. Lee J. Sanders, "From Thebes to Toronto and the 21st Century: An Incredible Journey," *Diabetes Spectrum*, 15:56–60, 2003, <http://spectrum.diabetesjournals.org/cgi/content/full/15/1/56> (December 20, 2007).

3. "History of Diabetes: From Raw Quinces & Gruel to Insulin," *Diabetes Health*, November 1, 1992, <http://www.diabeteshealth.com/read/1992/11/02/25.html> (December 20, 2007).

4. "Insulin: A Canadian Medical Miracle of the 20th Century," Sir Frederick Banting Legacy Foundation, <http://www.discoveryofinsulin.com/Introduction.htm> (December 27, 2007).

5. Joan MacCracken, "From Ants to Analogues: Puzzles and Promises in Diabetes Management," *Postgraduate Medicine,* April, 1997, <http://www.postgradmed.com/issues/1997/04_97/diabetes.htm> (December 28, 2007).

6. Melissa Sattley, "The History of Diabetes," *Diabetes Health*, November 1, 1996, <http://www.diabeteshealth.com/read/1996/11/01/715.html> (December 28, 2007).

7. *The Johns Hopkins White Papers: Diabetes,* Baltimore, Maryland: Johns Hopkins Medicine, 2007, pp. 57–58.

8. MacCracken.

## Chapter 4: Preventing Diabetes

1. International Diabetes Federation, "Did You Know?"
   <http://www.idf.org/home/index.cfm?unode=3B96906B-C026-2FD3-
   87B73F80BC22682A> (October 17, 2007).

2. National Diabetes Information Clearinghouse, "National Diabetes Statistics,"
   NIH Publication No. 06-3892, November 2005,
   <http://diabetes.niddk.nih.gov/dm/pubs/statistics> (January 23, 2008) and
   "Diabetes Rates Are Increasing among Youth," NIH News, November 13, 2007,
   <www.nih.gov/news/pr/nov2007/niddk-13.htm> (December 2, 2007).

3. "New Study Seeks to Lower Diabetes Risk in Youth," NIH News, August 28,
   2006, <http://www.nih.gov/news/pr/aug2006/niddk_28.htm> (January 23, 2008).

4. Ibid.

5. *The Johns Hopkins White Papers: Diabetes,* (Baltimore, Maryland: Johns Hopkins
   Medicine, 2007), p. 7.

6. National Diabetes Information Clearinghouse, "Diabetes Prevention Program,"
   NIH Publication No. 06-5099, August, 2006,
   <http://diabetes.niddk.nih.gov/dm/pubs/preventionprogram> (January 3, 2008).

7. Harvard School of Public Health, "Simple Steps to Preventing Diabetes,"
   <www.hsph.harvard.edu/nutritionsoiurce/diabetes.html> (October, 2007).

8. Ibid.

9. *The Johns Hopkins White Papers,* p. 7.

10. *American Diabetes Association Complete Guide to Diabetes*, 4th edition, (New
    York: Bantam, 2006), pp. 22–23.

11. Jo Cavallo, "Who Has Diabetes?" *JDRF Countdown*, Spring, 2006,
    <www.searchfordiabetes.org/public/documentscountdown.pdf> (October, 2007).

12. Ibid.

13. *The Johns Hopkins White Papers,* p. 11.

14. *American Diabetes Association Complete Guide to Diabetes,* p. 4.

15. Interview with Tesch West, January 20, 2008.

16. Ibid.

17. Ibid.

18. Ibid.

19. Ibid.

## Chapter 5: Testing and Treatment

1. *American Diabetes Association Complete Guide to Diabetes*, 4th edition, (New York: Bantam, 2006), p. 8.

2. *The Johns Hopkins White Papers: Diabetes*, (Baltimore, Maryland: Johns Hopkins Medicine, 2007, p. 16; and the National Diabetes Information Clearinghouse, "Diagnosis of Diabetes," National Institutes of Health, <http://diabetes.niddk.nih.gov/dm/pubs/diagnosis> (October 29, 2007).

3. Ibid.

4. *The Johns Hopkins White Papers: Diabetes*, p. 36.

5. Interview with Brian Hadley, January 17, 2008.

6. Ibid.

7. Ibid.

8. Ibid.

9. The Organ Procurement and Transplantation Network, "Transplants in the U.S. by Region," <http://www.optn.org/latestData/rptData.asp> (January 16, 2008).

10. Ibid.

11. *The Johns Hopkins White Papers: Diabetes*, p. 58.

## Chapter 6: Outlook for the Future

1. PBS.org, A Science Odyssey: People and Discoveries, "Banting and Best Isolate Insulin," <http://www.pbs.org/wgbh/databank/entries/dm22in.html> (December 28, 2007).

2. "Inhaled Insulin Exubera Discontinued," *Diabetes Today*, October 19, 2007, <www.diabetes.org/diabetesnewsarticle.jsp?storyId=16189532& filename=20071019 and Exubra Web site, © 2007, Pfizer, Inc., <http://www. exubera.com/content/con_index.jsp?setShowOn=../content/con_index.jsp& setShowHighlightOn=../content/con_index.jsp> (January 18, 2008).

3. "The Seven System," DexCom, ©2007, http://www.dexcom.com/html/dexcom_products.html

4. *The Johns Hopkins White Papers*, p. 53; and Medtronic, "Medtronic Diabetes Corporate Overview," n.d., <http://wwwp.medtronic.com/Newsroom/News ReleaseDetails.do?itemId=1101850830145&lang=en_US > (January 18, 2008).

5. "FDA Issues Safety Alert on Avandia," *FDA News,* May, 21, 2007, <http://www.fda.gov/topics/NEWS/2007/NEW01636.html> (January 21, 2007).

6. National Diabetes Information Clearinghouse, "Pancreatic Islet Transplantation," NIH Publication No. 07-4693, March, 2007, <http://diabetes.niddk.nih.gov/dam/pubs/pancreaticislet/> (January 19, 2008).

7. DiabetesMine.com, "Closing the Loop," June 21, 2005, and "JDF Pushing Hard on Artificial Pancreas," March 12, 2006, <http://www.diabetesmine.com> (January 20, 2008).

8. Aliyah Baruchin, "Twins on Medical Odyssey after a Diagnosis of Diabetes," *New York Times,* November 20, 2007.

9. Ibid.

10. "Obesity Gene Discovered," *Medical New Today*, April 13, 2007, <http://www. medicalnewstoday.com/article/67666.php> and Timothy M. Frayling, "A Common Variant in the FTO Gene Is Associated with Body Mass Index and Predisposes to Childhood and Adult Obesity," published online April 12, 2007, Science DOI: 10:1126/science.1141634, (January 21, 2008).

11. Decode Genetics, "Type 2 Diabetes," <http://www.decodeme.com> (January 21, 2008).

12. National Institutes of Health, NIH News, "Study Tests Oral Insulin to Prevent Type 1 Diabetes," January 31, 2007, <http://www.nih.gov/news/pr/jan2007/ niddk-31.htm> (January 1, 2008).

13. University of Colorado at Denver and Health Sciences Center, "UCDHSC Researchers Discover Antibody Used to Detect Diabetes," October 15, 2007, <http://www.uchsc.edu/news/newsrelease/2007/oct/antibody.html> (November 19, 2007).

14. American Diabetes Association, "The Genetics of Diabetes," <http//:www. diabetes.org/genetics.jsp> (January 21, 2008).

15. International Diabetes Federation, "The Human, Social, and Economic Impact of Diabetes," <http://www.idf.org/home/index.cfm?node=41> (October 17, 2007).

16. American Diabetes Association, "Study Shows Sharp Rise in Cost of Diabetes Nationwide," Feb. 27, 2003, <http://diabetes.org/for-media/2003-press-releases/02-27-03.jsp> (January 24, 2008).

17. Centers for Disease Control and Prevention, "Diabetes: Disabling Disease to Double by 2050," May 24, 2007, <http:www. cdc.gov/nccdphp/publications/aag/ddt.htm> (October 29, 2007).


## Chapter 7: Living with Diabetes

1. Riva Greenberg, "Diabetes: The Thinking Person's Disease," *DiabetesHealth,* September 10, 2007, <http://www.diabeteshealth.com/read/2007/09/10/5424.html> (October 27, 2007).

2. *American Diabetes Association Complete Guide to Diabetes*, 4th edition, (New York: Bantam, 2006), pp. 434–436.

3. American Diabetes Association, "Safe at School Campaign," <http://www.diabetes.org/advocacy-and-legalresources/discrimination/schools/safeschool.jsp> (January 28, 2008).

4. Interview with Tesch West, January 20, 2008.

5. Interview with Jake Benner, January 15, 2008.

6. *American Diabetes Association Complete Guide to Diabetes,* p. 90, 358.

7. Juvenile Diabetes Research Foundation International, "Driving and Type 1 Diabetes," <http://www.jdrf.org/index.cfm?page_id=103661> (January 28, 2008).

8. Interview with Lori Benner, January 15, 2008.

9. Lori Benner.

10. Ibid.

11. Jake Benner.

12. Ibid.

13. Ibid.

14. *American Diabetes Association Complete Guide to Diabetes,* p. 411.

15. Interview with Anne Hadley, January 17, 2008.

16. Juvenile Diabetes Research Foundation International, "Diabulemia," July 26, 2007, <http://www.jdrf.org/index.cfm?fuseaction=home.viewPage&page_id= FDF69313-1279-CFD5-A79B429F10056B6F> (January 29, 2008).

17. Lori Benner.

# Glossary

**analog**—A synthetic (man-made) form of insulin created through genetic engineering.

**antibodies**—Protein molecules produced by white blood cells that attack and destroy "foreign" invaders in the body, such as viruses. If they mistake normal body cells (such as beta cells) for foreign and attack them, they are called **autoantibodies**.

**beta cells**—Cells located in the islets of Langerhans of the pancreas that produce and release insulin.

**blood glucose level**—The amount of glucose in the blood.

**carbohydrates**—Starches and sugars that are turned into glucose in the small intestine.

**clinical trials**—Studies that check or compare the effectiveness and safety of medicines or medical devices by testing them on large groups of people.

**control group**—Group in a clinical trial receiving a placebo.

**deciliter (dl)**—One-tenth of a liter (a liter is 1.0567 quarts). The amount of glucose in the blood is measured in milligrams/deciliter (mg/dl).

**dehydration**—Extreme loss of body water.

**diabetic ketoacidosis**—A life-threatening condition caused by a lack of insulin and high blood glucose levels.

**diabetes mellitus**—A disease in which the body either cannot produce insulin or cannot use it properly, resulting in high levels of glucose in the blood.

**fasting**—Going without food or liquids except water for a set amount of time. Required before most blood tests to diagnose diabetes.

**genes**—Chemicals that determine a person's outward traits and inward traits and are passed on from one generation to the next.

**gestational diabetes**—Diabetes that occurs when a woman is pregnant.

**glucose**—The body's energy source. Created when carbohydrates are broken down in the digestive system.

**glycemic index**—A system that ranks carbohydrate-containing foods by number, based on how they affect blood glucose levels.

**glycogen**—A complex carbohydrate produced from glucose and stored in the liver and muscles to use for energy between meals and during sleep.

**hormone**—Chemical substance made by the body that controls the function of certain cells or organs.

**hyperglycemia**—Dangerously high glucose levels (above 130 mg/dl when fasting and above 180 mg/dl two hours after a meal). Can cause coma and death.

**hypoglycemia**—Dangerously low blood glucose levels (under 70 mg/dl). Can cause coma and death.

**immunosuppressant drugs**—Drugs that prevent the immune system from rejecting transplanted organs.

**insulin**—A hormone made in the pancreas that enables the body to use glucose. Insulin is also a drug taken by people with diabetes when their bodies do not make insulin naturally.

**insulin resistance**—The condition in which the body can no longer use insulin to keep blood glucose levels normal; the most common cause of type 2 diabetes.

**islets of Langerhans**—Specialized tissue in the pancreas that contains five types of hormone-producing cells, including insulin-producing beta cells.

**ketones**—Chemicals produced when the body burns fats for energy instead of glucose.

**milligram (mg)**—One-thousandth of a gram. The amount of glucose in the blood is measured in milligrams/deciliter (mg/dl).

**obesity**—Extreme overweight; a risk factor for type 2 diabetes.

**overweight**—Being too heavy and having too much fat for one's height, gender, age, and frame. Although often defined in terms of BMI (body mass index) for adults, BMI is too simple a number to be used for defining children and teens as overweight or obese.

**placebo**—An inactive substance or "dummy" medicine often used in clinical trials. People getting the placebo are compared to those getting the real drug to test the effectiveness of the real drug against the power of suggestion.

**prediabetes**—High glucose levels (between 100–125 mg/dl) but not high enough to be considered diabetes (126 mg/dl or higher).

**risk**—A condition, behavior, or other element that increases the chance of developing a disease.

**stem cells**—Cells that can grow into any other type of cell in the body.

# For More Information

## Further Reading

Allman, Toney. *Diabetes*. New York: Chelsea House Publishers, 2008.

Lawton, Sandra Augustyn, ed. *Diabetes Information for Teens: Health Tips about Managing Diabetes and Preventing Related Complications Including Information About Insulin, Glucose Control, Healthy Eating, Physical Activity, and Learning to Live With Diabetes*. Detroit: Omnigraphics, 2006.

Moran, Katherine J. *Diabetes: The Ultimate Teen Guide*. Lanham, MD: The Scarecrow Press, 2007.

Parker, Katrina. *Living with Diabetes*. New York: Facts on File, 2007.

Yuwiler, Janice M. *Insulin*. Detroit: Lucent Books, 2005.

## Internet Addresses

*American Diabetes Association*. <**http://www.diabetes.org**>.

*Children with Diabetes*. ©1995–2008. <**http://www.chidrenwithdiabetes.com**>.

*Diabetes Mine*. <**http://www.diabetesmine.com/**>.

## Organizations

**American Diabetes Association**
1701 North Beauregard Street
Alexandria, VA 22311
(800) 342-2383
http://www.diabetes.org

**Centers for Disease Control and Prevention**
Division of Diabetes Translation
National Center for Chronic Disease Prevention and Health Promotion
4770 Buford Highway NE, Mailstop K-10
Atlanta, GA 30341-03717
(770) 488-5000
http://www.cdc.gov/diabetes

**International Diabetes Federation**
Avenue Emile De Mot 19
B-1000 Brussels
Belgium
+32-2-5385511
http://www.idf.org

**Juvenile Diabetes Research Foundation International**
120 Wall Street
New York, NY 10005-4001
(800) 533-2873
http://www.jdrf.org

**National Diabetes Education Program**
1 Diabetes Way
Bethesda, MD 20814-9692
(301) 496-3583
http://www.ndep.nih.gov

**National Diabetes Information Clearinghouse**
1 Information Way
Bethesda, MD 20892-3560
(800) 860-8747
http://www.diabetes.niddk.nih.gov/

**National Institute of Diabetes and Digestive and Kidney Disorders**
Office of Communications & Public Liaison
Building 31, Room9A06
31 Center Drive, MSC 2560
Bethesda, MD 20892-2560
(301) 496-3583
<http://www2.niddk.nih.gov>

# Index

medication, 8, 13, 18, 35–36, 38, 89, 93, 100, 129

metformin, 58, 66

multiple sclerosis, 30

## N

nausea, 44, 130

nephropathy, 38

nerve damage, 38, 136

neuropathy, 38–39

neutral protamine Hagedorn (NPH), 57

non–insulin–dependent diabetes, 31

numbness, 7, 34, 38, 131

nutrition, 20, 68, 79, 96, 101, 140

## O

obesity, 7, 17, 25, 32, 74–75, 115, 118

Oral Glucose Tolerance Test, 82–83

overweight, 16–18, 33, 35, 63–64, 66, 70, 74–75, 96–118

## P

pancreas, 8, 27–29, 32–33, 45–54, 57–58, 60, 64, 73, 85, 102–103, 108–109, 111–115, 119, 135

prediabetes, 25, 33, 66, 82–83, 117

pregnancy, 83, 132

prevention, 62, 65–66, 92, 115, 122

protamine zinc insulin (PZI), 57

## S

smoking, 37–39, 71, 134, 137

stem cells, 111–112, 155

stroke, 37, 122

synthetic insulin, 58

## T

Thompson, Leonard, 52–54

transplants, 60, 102–103, 111–114

type 1 diabetes, 7–8, 28–30, 32, 35–36, 38, 40, 49, 60, 62, 73–76, 78, 82, 84–85, 88, 91–92, 97–98, 100, 102, 105, 108, 111, 115–120, 125, 135, 140

type 2 diabetes, 7–9, 16, 18, 23, 25, 28, 31–36, 38, 58, 62–65, 68, 70–71, 73–75, 78–80, 82, 84–85, 88–89, 91–92, 94, 96, 100, 108–109, 114–115, 117–118, 123–124, 129–131

## U

United States Department of Agriculture (USDA), 24, 67–70

University of Alberta in Edmonton Canada, 60, 112

University of Minnesota, 60

urination, 7, 15, 30, 34–35, 31, 34–35, 42, 45, 61, 79, 94, 140

## W

weight loss, 7, 15, 31, 34–35, 42, 65–66, 95, 140

white blood cells, 39, 157